The perjury trial of Patrick   , Co. Clare

Maynooth Studies in Local History

SERIES EDITOR Michael Potterton

The six volumes in the MSLH series for 2024 cover a broad chronological and geographical canvas across four provinces, focusing variously on people, places, families, communities and events. It begins with an unlikely search for Vikings in the north-west of Ireland, where the evidence is more compelling than most people realize. Further south, in Carrick-on-Shannon, we trace the fortunes of the St George family from the Plantation of Leitrim through to the decades after the Famine. From Carrick we continue south to Ballymurray in Roscommon and its Quaker community (1717–1848), including their relationship with the Croftons of Mote Park. Further south still, in 1701 Jacobite Patrick Hurly of Moughna, Co. Clare, was at the centre of a 'sham robbery' of gold and jewellery worth about €500,000 in today's money. Unlike Hurly, Mary Mercer was renowned for her charitable endeavours, including the establishment of a shelter for orphaned girls in Dublin three hundred years ago in 1724. Finally, the last volume in this year's crop examines the evolution of the resilient farming community at Carbury in Co. Kildare.

* * *

Raymond Gillespie passed away after a very short illness on 8 February 2024. He had established the Maynooth Studies in Local History (MSLH) series with Irish Academic Press in 1995, from which time he served as series editor for a remarkable 27 years and 153 volumes. Taking over those editorial reins in 2021, my trepidation was tempered by the knowledge that Raymond agreed to remain as an advisor. True to his word, he continued to recommend contributors, provide peer-review, mentor first-time authors (and series editors) and give sound advice. Shoes that seemed big to fill in 2021 just got a lot bigger.

Maynooth Studies in Local History: Number 170

The perjury trial of Patrick Hurly of Moughna, Co. Clare: elite Catholic responses to the emerging Protestant ascendancy

Brendan Twomey

FOUR COURTS PRESS

Set in 11.5pt on 13.5pt Bembo by
Carrigboy Typesetting Services for
FOUR COURTS PRESS LTD
7 Malpas Street, Dublin 8, Ireland
www.fourcourtspress.ie
and in North America for
FOUR COURTS PRESS
c/o IPG, 814 N Franklin Street, Chicago, IL 60610

© Brendan Twomey and Four Courts Press 2024

ISBN 978-1-80151-133-9

All rights reserved. Without limiting the rights under copyright reserved alone, no part of this publication may be reproduced, stored in or introduced into a retrieval system, or transmitted, in any form or by any means (electronic, mechanical, photocopying, recording or otherwise), without the prior written permission of both the copyright owner and the above publisher of this book.

Printed in Ireland
by Sprint Books, Dublin

Contents

Acknowledgments 6
Editorial conventions 6
Introduction 9
1 Protestant ascendancy: consolidating conquest and winning the peace 17
2 Guilty as charged? The trial and conviction of Patrick Hurly 26
3 The case of Patrick Hurly in law, in politics and in print 56
Conclusion 74
Notes 80
Abbreviations 80
Index 84

FIGURES
1 Signature of Patrick Hurly 7
2 Affidavit of Patrick Hurly 10
3 File note on certificate of Hurly debts 36
4 Certificate of Hurly debts 36
5 Note of Hurly's testimony 43
6 Report on death of Hurly 49
7 Title page of *Tryal* 51
8 Title page of *Appendix* 52
9 Title page of *Innocence Justify'd* 53
10 Sir Donat O'Brien 57

Acknowledgments

My first and most important acknowledgment must be to the late and much missed Prof. Raymond Gillespie, my good friend, historical mentor, and lunch companion of more than twenty years. Ray was the lead professor for my MA in Local History in Maynooth in 2002. This experience was my gateway to the world of historical research. Ray was also the editor of my two previous volumes in the Maynooth Studies in Local History series. On our regular lunch dates (there were many) we would earnestly discuss and of course solve all of Ireland's outstanding historical issues and vexed questions for all periods, including (maybe especially) for those periods and topics that were beyond our immediate areas of expertise!

Others have helped me in many ways, great and small, in putting this book together; their help has been much appreciated. In particular I would like to thank especially John Bergin, Andrew Carpenter, David Hayton, James Kelly, Brian O'Dalaigh, Liam O'Rourke, and Patrick Walsh. I also would like to express my appreciation to Michael Potterton, the current editor of the Maynooth Studies in Local History series, for his forbearance for the 'missed' deadlines and the late requests to include the latest nugget of 'just discovered' (more usually just fully appreciated) information.

Finally, I would like to, as ever, express my thanks to my wife Valerie for her endless patience in putting up with yet another round of seemingly never-ending days and nights where I was locked away in the study working on this text.

EDITORIAL CONVENTIONS

Dates: All dates are given in the old style, though the year is taken to begin on 1 January rather than 25 March. Dates have been presented as they are found in the sources though if only the old style was used the new style has been provided.

Acknowledgments

Notes: Most of the details of the alleged 'sham' robbery and the subsequent trial of Patrick Hurly are taken from three sources: the pamphlets that were published in Dublin in 1701, the Inchiquin Papers in the National Library of Ireland, and the state papers. Listing a specific endnote for each detail taken from these sources would result in dozens of individual references. The original source for details mentioned in the text can be accessed by searching in the relevant source. In the trial text this would be under the name of the witness and in the Inchiquin and the state papers by the date of the item mentioned in the text.

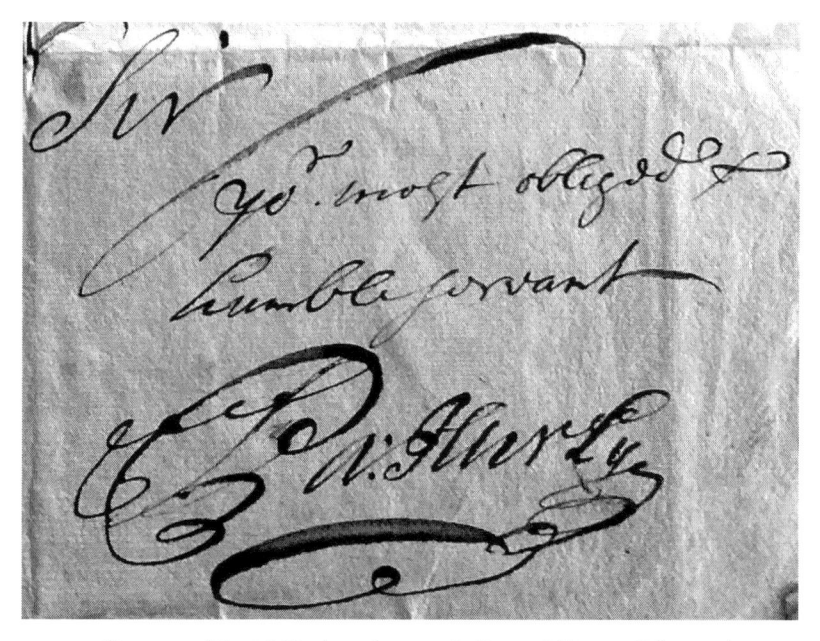

1. Signature of Patrick Hurly on letter to Sir Donat O'Brien, 5 Feb. 1697/8 (source: NLI Inchiquin Papers MS 45,325/1)

Spellings: In the eighteenth century the most usual spelling of the townland where the robbery took place was Moughna, and this spelling has been used throughout, except when citing directly from a contemporary source where the original spelling has been retained. There are numerous variations for the spelling of the name Hurly in the contemporary sources including Hurley, which is the most common modern spelling. He signed himself Hurly, which was also the most frequent contemporary spelling (fig. 1). Accordingly,

Hurly has been used throughout except when citing directly from a contemporary source where the original spelling has been retained. There are numerous variations of the spelling of Donat's name in the contemporary sources; these include Donagh and Donough. There are also numerous spelling variants of the family name O'Brien, including O'Bryan and O'Brian. The most frequent contemporary spelling for his name was Donat O'Brien and this has been used throughout except when citing directly from a contemporary source. Citations from contemporary sources such as pamphlets, newspapers and letters have retained the original spelling and orthography without highlighting old-style spelling and obvious errors.

Introduction

On 31 May 1701, the former mid-ranking Jacobite functionary, Patrick Hurly (*c*.1666–1716) of Moughna, Co. Clare, described as a Gentleman, was found guilty of perjury at the court of king's bench in Dublin; he was fined £100. The jury reached this judgment following a day-long trial in which they were presented with a great mass of complex and contested evidence; the jury only deliberated for half an hour. Hurly was convicted of having sworn a false affidavit in respect of what was termed at the trial a 'sham robbery' (fig. 2). His affidavit was sworn before Dean Neptune Blood, a local JP in Ennis, and dated 6 March 1700, only three days after the alleged robbery. In the affidavit, Hurly recounted in dramatic detail how, on the evening of Sunday 3 March 1700, at least four heavily armed men wearing greatcoats and with their faces hidden by masks, had burst into his father's house in rural Moughna, how they had tied him and his visitor Mr Ronane to the bedpost in his bed chamber and imprisoned his household servants, how they had ransacked the house, how they had fired several shots and, finally, how they had made good their escape. He claimed that the raiders had stolen several hundred gold coins, jewellery and other goods to the value of £1,300: a minimum of €500,000 in today's money. (The daily wage for an unskilled labourer in this period was 6*d*. or less than £8 per annum.) The robbery, whether sham or real, had taken place at Hurly's father's substantial farmhouse. In addition to the perjury charge, Hurly and four of his associates were also convicted of attempting to defraud the 'popish inhabitants' of Clare by seeking compensation under the provisions of the Act for the Better Suppression of Tories, Robbers and Rapparees: and for Preventing Robberies Burglaries and Other Heinous Crimes.[1] A provision in this act had decreed that where a robbery had been carried out by 'Papists', or those 'Reputed of the Popish Religion, the Popish Inhabitants there shall make satisfaction'. In his affidavit Hurly had declared that the raiders 'by the tone of their voice he believed to be Irish-men and papists'. The sentence for the fraud conviction

Com Clare. The Information of Patrick Hurly of Moghna in y.e s.d
County gentl. taken before me Neptune Blood, Deane of
Killfenora, one of his Maties Justices of y.e Peace for y.e s.d County
The said Inform.t being duely sworne on y.e holy Evangelist, & Examined,
saith, that on Sunday the third of March one thousand
six hundred and Ninety Nine, about Eleaven of y.e Clock
att Night being then att his ffathers house in Moghna
aforesaid, and in his Chamber, he saw three Men arm'd
burst in an out Doors of y.e said house, which opened
into a Garden, & threw Downe m.r John Ronane, who
then was user y.e said Doore; & in a rude manner with
swords & Pistols in their hands Entred into y.e s.d Chamber
dragging the said m.r Ronane with them, & Instantly
there appeared a fourth person arm'd, & with their faces
masqued, & makeing a shott att this Inform.t, they
Imediatly tyed him & the said m.r Ronane with cords
fast to a Bedstead; calling this Informant Rogue, Rascall,
sonne of a whore, treacherous Villane to his Country, &
many abusive words to that effect. This s.d Inform.t
further saith, that the said p.sons by the tone of their
speech seemed to be Irish Men, and beleives them to
be Papists, but knowes not any one of them either
by their Names or p.sons, that Imediatly they broke
open three large Truncks, and tooke out of one of y.e
said Truncks a Bagg, wherein were three hundred
seventy & four Guineas, and three hundred fourty
five Pistoles, amounting in all to y.e Summe of Eight

2. Affidavit of Patrick Hurly, sworn before David Bindon, 16 May 1699
(source: NLI Inchiquin Papers MS 45,334/3)

is not recorded in the archives. Within days of the alleged robbery the authorities, in the first instance in Clare and shortly afterwards at the highest level in the criminal legal system in Dublin up to the lords justices, formed the firm opinion that no real robbery had taken place. They were convinced that the entire escapade was an elaborate hoax carried out by Hurly so as to facilitate a claim for compensation under the 'rapparee acts'. Such an egregious affront to the recently re-established, and still not fully secure, 'Protestant ascendancy' could not be countenanced; not only because the alleged claim was for such a vast sum, but perhaps more significantly because it was being perpetrated by a well-known Catholic Jacobite personality, and one with a less-than-clean reputation, at a local, national and even international level to boot.[2]

By the end of March 1700, a mere three weeks after the alleged robbery, Patrick Hurly had been arrested and he remained in gaol, first in Ennis and then in Dublin, until his trial at the court of king's bench in Dublin fourteen months later. In the eighteenth century most criminal prosecutions were private affairs; essentially victims had to undertake the sometimes very difficult task of gathering the evidence and pursuing a prosecution. The Hurly trial was different. In this instance, the authorities treated the prosecution as a state matter, and so the case became Rex v. Hurly. In the period between the alleged robbery and the trial, the authorities in Clare, then in Dublin, and eventually in London, had engaged in an unusually extensive and complex pre-trial investigation process. On the day of the trial the prosecution team was led by the two most senior Irish law officers: the Attorney General Alan Brodrick MP (1656–1728) and the Solicitor General Robert Rochfort MP (1652–1727). The trial of Patrick Hurly was much more than a local affair. Over the course of the winter of 1700, and through the early months of 1701, the Hurly issue became something of a contemporary legal, political and print *cause célèbre* in Ireland. This was because within days of the robbery, and operating from his various prison cells, Hurly had launched a parallel legal process in which he made serious allegations of treason and Jacobite conspiracy against the local Clare magnet and MP Sir Donat O'Brien of Dromoland (1642–1717). Hurly's allegations had the effect of raising what initially may have appeared to be just a local matter of an alleged armed robbery and fraud in rural Co. Clare, into a national political affair and one which had an unusually large and important presence in the nascent world of Irish print.

The Hurly affair resulted in the production of five separate publications in 1701.³ At an unknown date but sometime before the trial, Hurly published a to-date unrecovered pamphlet entitled *Patrick Hurly's vindication with some remarkable passages of his life and actions* (hereafter *Hurly's vindication*). In this pamphlet Hurly not only gave his side of the story of the robbery but he also made his allegations of treason against O'Brien. Some months after the trial a fifty-six-page pamphlet entitled *The tryal and conviction of Patrick Hurly: late of Moughna in the county of Clare, Gent. In his majesty's court of kings' bench in Ireland, the 31st of May 1701* (hereafter *Tryal*) was published in Dublin and in London. This pamphlet appeared to be a full transcript of the trial. Simultaneously with the publication of the *Tryal* an anonymous pamphlet entitled *An appendix being an answer to a Libel intitled Patrick Hurly's vindication* (hereafter *Appendix*) was also published in Dublin. Both the *Tryal* and the *Appendix* were printed at the behest of, and almost certainly with the financial support of O'Brien. Finally, towards the end of 1701 Hurly published a response to the *Appendix* entitled *Innocence Justify'd; or, the correction of an infamous libel, called the tryal & conviction of Patrick Hurly &c. published without license by Gunn, Whalley &c. together, with a direct Paragraphical answer, to a most scandalour [sic] pamphlet, entituled The Appendix &c. suppos'd to be writ by order of Sir Donogh O'Bryen* (hereafter *Innocence Justify'd*). The details contained in these pamphlets, and especially in the *Tryal*, constitute the primary sources for the events recounted in this book.

The case against Hurly advanced by the prosecution team as set out in the *Tryal* seems quite straightforward. Hurly was presented as a thorough rogue and a serial cheat. Evidence was given in court to show how, in the period prior to the robbery, he was in desperate financial straits, he was hiding out in Clare and he was in constant fear of being 'blocked up' (imprisoned) by some of his numerous creditors. The prosecution team presented the robbery as nothing more than a criminal scheme aimed at recovering his fortune. Hurly's case, as set out in *Hurly's vindication*, reiterated in *Innocence Justify'd* and presented by his defence counsel on the day of the trial, was that he was a man of substance, that there had been a real armed robbery, that the alleged perpetrators, all of whom were either his servants or his relatives, had been suborned by threats of hanging and by bribes, and that the whole affair was nothing more than a plot by O'Brien to ruin and discredit him. If the only corpus of evidence for the Hurly affair, and indeed for the life and times of Patrick Hurly, was the text of the *Tryal*, and the further details contained in the other pamphlets, then the entire imbroglio could be considered a mere local historical curiosity that somehow had become the subject of a minor, albeit very interesting, pamphlet war. It could be presented as a mere footnote, a colourful example of an armed robbery, even if for a rather large sum, that had been perpetrated by rapparees/Tories who had perhaps inadvertently targeted one of their own. Alternatively, and as alleged by the prosecution team, the Hurly affair could be seen as a 'sham robbery' and an attempted fraud that had been carried out by a Catholic/Jacobite desperado and member of the displaced Catholic elite. Indeed, this is primarily how the few references to the trial of Hurly have been represented in the historiography of the period to date. For example, the Hurly case made a modest appearance in Thomas Wright's 1854 *History of Ireland* where, in a discussion of the post-war unrest which Wright termed 'the slow scattered war carried on between the government and the rapparees', Hurly's escapade was described as a 'remarkable example' of actions where the unscrupulous 'took advantage of the condition of the people, to perform, under cover of the laws against rapparees and the penal statutes, acts which were no less barbarous and unjust'.[4] In his influential 1956 study of the Williamite land confiscations, the leading historian J.G. Simms simply called Hurly 'an extraordinary adventurer' and 'an unsavoury character'.[5] In 1983 the leading Irish-born English jurist James Comyn included a summary of the Hurly case in his compendium of notable Irish legal cases. He made some interesting observations on the technical and evidentiary procedures used in the trial and he reached a somewhat similar conclusion to Simms in respect of the character of the defendant.[6] To date, the only relatively full treatment of the Hurly case has been a 1993 article entitled 'The Moughna affair, 1699 [sic], and the bizarre career of Patrick Hurley' by Ciarán Ó Murchadha from *The Other Clare* where Hurly was characterized as 'an informer'.[7] In this particular case, however, we are fortunate that, in addition to the printed sources listed above, there are two voluminous sources of additional corroborative and credible evidence that provide a great deal of extra information on the behind-the-scenes developments in the fifteen months between the alleged robbery in early March 1700 and the trial at the end of May 1701. This additional evidence comes first from the file of more that three hundred items on the Hurly affair that was created by O'Brien and which is preserved in the Inchiquin Papers in the National Library of Ireland.[8] O'Brien had very good reason to create such a file. Within days of his arrest Hurly commenced a high-profile campaign against O'Brien accusing him of treason during the war over a decade earlier and, perhaps more importantly, he accused O'Brien of continuing his Jacobite conspiratorial activities especially during the recent invasion scares of 1692 and 1695. There is no doubt that for a time in late 1700 as a result of Hurly's allegations O'Brien was under severe legal and political pressure and he was even arrested briefly in Dublin in December 1700. The Hurly affair was also of sufficient import to feature prominently in the state papers from the period where again the focus of attention was on investigating Hurly's allegations of treason against O'Brien.[9]

While Patrick Hurly may be the central figure in the events described in this book, the figure of Sir Donat O'Brien is also ever-present. Some of Hurly's reputed escapades stretch the bounds of improbability, almost to breaking point. Over the course of a three-decade career, both before and after what were later referred to as his 'troubles and misfortunes' in 1701, Hurly was allegedly involved in a series of financial dealings of questionable legality. These included accusations of serial embezzlement, particularly targeted at Protestants while he was a revenue collector for the Jacobite regime in Dublin and later in Limerick/Galway during the war and later again when he acted as the agent for Irish regiments in France after the defeat of the Jacobite forces in Ireland in 1691.[10] The locations involved in Hurly's various 'difficulties' ranged from Dublin to London, Paris and Holland. Hurly was accused of operating under numerous aliases, including representing himself as the fictitious Viscount Mountcallan, to say nothing of his numerous amorous adventures and bigamous relationships, and his reputed '40 wives' as alleged in his death notice in a Dublin newspaper in January 1716.[11] As one follows the evidential trail of the Hurly case, however, other important Catholic figures, or first-generation converts – what could be termed 'crypto-Catholics' – come increasingly into focus and in this context the second major figure at the heart of this drama is Sir Donat O'Brien, 1st Baron Inchiquin, The O'Briens, who claimed descent from the Irish king Brian Boru, were one of the oldest and most respected families in Clare. Donat was the son of Conor O'Brien of Leamaneh (1617–51) and Máire Rua Mac Mahon (1616–86); he was just 9 when his father was killed in a skirmish with Cromwellian troops in 1651. Shortly afterwards, in a stratagem clearly aimed at preserving the family estates, his mother married her third husband John Cooper, a Cromwellian soldier. In 1663, Donat was declared an innocent papist, thereby copper-fastening his family's retention of their estates. He was the first member of his branch of the family to conform to the established church and was created baronet in 1686.

This book presents the evidence for Hurly's trial and conviction as recorded in the published pamphlets and supported by the evidence extracted from the Inchiquin Papers and the state papers. It seeks to answer a series of questions surrounding this incident. First, was Hurly guilty of perjury and the attempted fraud as charged? Did the evidence stack up? And did Hurly receive a fair trial? Second, why was it so important to the powers that be, both in Clare and in Dublin, to secure the conviction of a mid-level Jacobite rogue for an alleged robbery and an attempted fraud that had occurred in a remote part of rural Clare? Third, why were both sides in this dispute so intent on having their side of the story preserved in print? The publication of four separate pamphlets in Dublin in 1701, including what had the appearance of a full transcript of a criminal trial, was one of the first, if not *the* first Irish-based and non-theological pamphlet war. Fourthly, where does the story of the trial and conviction of Hurly fit into the actions and stratagems of the displaced/dispossessed Catholic elite in the early decades of the Protestant ascendancy? Finally, what can the unusually detailed evidence provided by the *Tryal* text and the corroborative detail from the Inchiquin and state papers tell us about the working of contemporary Irish criminal investigation and court procedures? Irish historiography has perhaps been guilty of not paying sufficient attention to the evidentiary minutiae of criminal trials, and especially to those such as the Hurly trial which had an obvious political edge. The tendency has been to regard such trials as being irredeemably rigged in favour of the prosecution and to treat them as merely another manifestation of a coercive colonial state. Francis Bernard, Hurly's defence counsel, claimed 'these prosecutions have been carried on by bribery, and such like practices'. Issues considered in this instance include accusations of physical and psychological pressure on witnesses, impersonation of witnesses, manoeuvring to have the case held in an alternative venue and therefore beyond the influence of major local interests, the organization of numerous searches, the taking of numerous affidavits, the legal and procedural guidance provided by the judge to the jury, and the use of an interpreter to facilitate testimony from monoglot Irish speakers. Recent work on the eighteenth-century Irish criminal system, especially that of Neal Garnham, has painted a more nuanced picture, demonstrating its pervasiveness and its penetration into local affairs, taking account of the large numbers involved, and its less than totally hegemonic presence in eighteenth-century Ireland, and away from simplistic representations of it as a system of naked elite coercion or arbitrary power.[12] As averred by S.J. Connolly when examining the legal and criminal world of eighteenth-century Ireland, 'the main basis of social order must be sought in some variation on the themes of deference and hegemony'.[13]

This book is divided into three chapters and a brief conclusion. Chapter 1 sets the scene nationally and locally. It briefly addresses a series of actions taken by the Protestant ascendancy in the first two decades after the Jacobite/Williamite wars in areas of security, courts and land settlement, which impacted directly on the Hurly trial. Chapter 2 reviews the evidence for the prosecution and the defence, and the behind-the-scenes activities of all parties as presented in the published trial text and in the pamphlets, the Inchiquin Papers and the state papers. Chapter 3 assesses the way in which the trial played out in contemporary law, politics and print. The book ends with some brief conclusions.

1. Protestant ascendancy: consolidating conquest and winning the peace

For the recently re-established Protestant elite, the situation in Ireland at the dawn of the eighteenth century was simultaneously full of dangers and full of possibilities. The privations of war and the near-loss of their estates to the revanchist Catholic interest was only a decade in the past, and it remained vividly fresh in the memory.[1] Following the third military victory over the forces of Gaelic and Catholic Ireland, the Protestant ascendancy were determined to do all in their power to cement their position within this new dispensation; and this time they were determined to make it permanent. Having won the hard-fought war, with English military support, a fact that was acknowledged and resented in equal measure, they set out with renewed determination to do whatever was necessary at a local and a national level to win the peace. Conversely, from the perspective of Patrick Hurly and his fellow members of the deposed Roman Catholic gentry and elite, the world could be a very dark place. Only a decade earlier many, perhaps most of them, including Hurly had been active participants in a fully functioning Catholic regime, a regime that was extending Catholic interest and control into almost all aspects of Irish life, a regime that was bent on reversing the Cromwellian and Restoration land settlements, and thereby permanently vanquishing their Protestant successors. These hopes had been dashed by the military defeat at the hands of the Protestant forces of William III. Two recent studies of this period – Patrick Walsh's *The making of the Irish Protestant ascendancy: the life of William Conolly, 1662–1729* (2010) and Eoin Kinsella's *Catholic survival in Protestant Ireland, 1660–1711: Colonel John Browne, landownership and the Articles of Limerick* (2018) – perfectly capture the differing perspectives, options and stratagems available to the elites on either side, in the decades after the conclusion of the war in 1691.[2] In this febrile and contested atmosphere, fortunes could be made and lost.

In pursuit of the strategy of winning the peace, the 1690s had witnessed the only partial ratification of the treaty terms and, starting in 1695, the Irish parliament had enacted a series of anti-Catholic measures, soon to be termed the Penal Laws. By 1700 laws restricting Catholics' right to foreign education, intermarriage with Protestants, rights of Catholic solicitors to practice, strictures on the episcopal structures of the Roman Catholic church and presenting Catholics with unacceptable oaths, had already been enacted. Most Catholics suspected, correctly as it turned out, that worse might follow. What were the Catholic elite to do? They were forced to face the world as it really was and not as it had been or as they would wish it to be. The new landowning elite of Protestant adventurers, soldiers or investors may have been looked upon with hauteur by the bardic spokespersons of the deposed Catholic elite of Daniel Corkery's 'hidden Ireland', but this new landowning class constituted the actual boots on the ground.[3] One option was to actively participate in what increasingly seemed to be a doomed, pointless and localized neo-guerrilla resistance of rapparees and Tories – Wright's 'slow scattered war'. A second option was to participate in the apparently never-ending, informer-ridden and at times incompetent Jacobite plots emanating from the exiled court in St Germaine – Éamonn Ó Ciardha's 'fatal attraction'. For many, however, and especially for those who stayed in Ireland after the end of the war, the preferred option was to transfer their energies and their money from the military to the political arena. This trend, already evident in the last years of the pre-war Restoration period, perforce meant that these Catholic landowners became at least passive if not active supporters of the new regime, keen to use its legal mechanism to preserve their patrimony.[4] The reality therefore was that even at the end of this disastrous century for the Gaelic and Catholic leadership there remained a distinct and important cohort of Catholic landowners who in many parts of the country retained significant wealth and important social (if declining political) standing. In addition, there were numerous first- and second-generation convert landowners; what could be termed crypto-Catholic landowners. Donat O'Brien was a typical example of these first-generation Protestants. For both groups preserving

Protestant ascendancy: consolidating conquest and winning the peace

their lands required expert legal advice and valid paperwork. Unsurprisingly, this situation resulted in a rash of petitions to have outlawries revoked, numerous private acts of parliament to address specific situations and, in due course, complex often decades-long and intergenerational court cases. Catholic opinion, both in Ireland and in the exiled court in France, was divided on how far elite Catholics should use such legal stratagems to accommodate themselves to the new dispensation.[5] Those Catholics who were on the margins of the landowning fold, the eighteenth-century equivalent of the men of no property, had fewer options. The subsequent actions of opportunists such as Hurly and Redmond Joy (discussed in Chapter 3), both of whom came from within this cadre (informers in some eyes), do not always fit easily into the traditional narrative of dispossession and of enduring, resolute and heroic resistance. This chapter does not rehearse this well-researched ground in any further detail; rather, it briefly discusses three areas in which the Protestant ascendancy sought to assert its newfound power and which had a direct impact on the working out of Hurly case: security policy, control of the courts and confirmation of landownership.

SECURITY: TORIES, RAPPAREES AND JACOBITES

The defeat of the Jacobite army and the signing of the Treaty of Limerick in October 1691 finally ended the war in Ireland. There were several other treaties/articles of agreement the most important of which were the articles of Galway which had been signed some months earlier. Hurly claimed that he qualified under the provisions of the articles of Galway, although this was disputed by one of the witnesses during the trial who claimed that Hurly was already in France on the qualifying date. Apparently, Hurly was successful in his appeal for the reversal of his outlawry. Not surprisingly, privations and mayhem caused by rapparees/Tories had thrived during the wartime conditions of 1689–91 and scattered and sporadic local resistance continued for at least a decade. Enhancing security and enforcing law and order, into even the most remote parts of the country, was therefore near the top of the agenda for the leadership of the Protestant political nation; now represented more than ever by the MPs in the Dublin parliament. Given the symbolic importance that became attached to the Hurly case, it is not surprising to note that four leading lawyers, all of whom were MPs, were involved in the prosecution team during the Hurly trial.

In addition to the explicitly anti-Catholic 'penal' legislation discussed above, in the three decades following the conclusion of the Williamite wars the Irish parliament passed six acts aimed at the suppression of Tories and rapparees as well as issuing numerous proclamations against named Tories and rapparees.[6] A centrepiece of this legislation was the 1695 Act for the Better Suppression of Tories, Robbers and Rapparees: and for Preventing Robberies Burglaries and Other Heinous Crimes. In language typical of the time, the opening paragraph of the act declared:

> Forasmuch as by the late rebellion in this kingdom, a great part thereof hath been left waste and desolate; and the frequent robberies, murders and other notorious felonies committed by robbers, rapparees and Tories, upon their keeping, hath greatly discouraged the re-planting of this kingdom, the Papist inhabitants thereof, chusing rather to suffer strangers to be robbed and despoiled of their goods, than to apprehend or convict the offenders, of whom the greatest part are people of the same country; and countenanced, harboured and concealed by the inhabitants thereof. For the remedy of which mischiefs, and for the better encouragement of strangers to plant and inhabit this Your Majesty's Kingdom of *Ireland,* and for the general preservation of peace and property of Your Majesty's good subjects therein.[7]

The act went on to specify that 'the inhabitants of every barony or county, within this kingdom, shall make full satisfaction for all robberies, burglaries, burning of houses or haggards of corn, killing or mayming of cattel, which shall be done, by robber, rapparees or Tories'. It continued that if the above had been carried out by 'Papists, or reputed of the popish religion, the popish inhabitants there shall make satisfaction; and if by Protestants, or reputed Protestants, then the Protestant inhabitants there to make satisfaction'. While this act had a *prima facie* appearance of being even-handed, in that the sanguinary financial burden would be levied on the community from which the perpetrators had come, the clear expectation was that the penalty provisions would, in most instances, apply to Roman Catholics. These provisions can also perhaps be construed as another example of actions within the legal system to encourage the residual Catholic landowning elite/gentry to convert to the established church and thereby avoid such an imposition, which would have had the collateral benefit of reinforcing state authority at a local level. The victims of such rapparee or Tory robberies were required to report the details of the crime by 'Examination upon oath ... before some justice of the peace' within four days of the event and if they knew the persons involved to complete 'bond by recognizance to prosecute the offender or offenders, by indictment, or otherwise, according to law'. The schedule of losses was to be presented to the grand jury at the next assizes or quarter-sessions, which, on approval, would levy the relevant charge. It was these provisions that Hurly sought to use to his advantage by swearing his affidavit of 6 March and later by lodging his (unsuccessful, as it transpired) claim for £1,300 compensation from the popish inhabitants of Clare at the Ennis assizes. The 1695 act was to continue in force for three years (sunset clauses were a common feature of legislation passed in this period) and in 1697 the act was renewed for a further seven years.[8] The paucity of assizes records means that it is not clear how many claims for compensation under the rapparee acts were claimed and paid out in this period. One recorded example is the case of James Fontaine's lengthy and colourful description of his encounter with French privateers and local Tories – the so-called Huguenot hero of Berhaven in 1704. Fontaine claimed that he was able to 'prove the facts to the satisfaction of the Grand Jury for the country of Cork ... and that there were many Irishmen among the assailants ... and after examination awarded me £800, to be paid by the county of Cork in conformity with the act of parliament'.[9] A central assertion of the prosecution case against Hurly, as stated by the solicitor-general in his opening statement, was that Hurly was familiar with the detailed provisions of these acts and he had boasted that 'by the act of parliament, if he could fix a robbery on the country, he could tax what sum he pleased'. Evidence was also given by Capt. Lynch, the Hurlys' landlord, as to how Hurly had enquired of him in respect of a claim for such compensation made by a Mr Banks, who had been robbed of £250, and for which 'the grand jury, at the assizes, allow'd him the money when he petition'd for it'.

While rapparees posed a serious, if not quite an existential, internal threat to the new Protestant ascendancy, conspiratorial Jacobitism emanating from the exiled court of St Germain in France certainly posed an ever-present external existential threat. In this febrile and fearful environment, assertions that that the residual Catholic elite, and the convert wings of their families, were a permanent and potentially treasonous force in residence could gain a ready hearing. In addition, for decades after 1691 the Irish regiments in the French army were represented by Irish Jacobites, and by French and English propogandists, as constituting the potential core of a Jacobite invasion force that might be unleashed to restore the rightful king as and when French naval successes in the English Channel and the Irish Sea would allow. The burning of the French fleet at La Hogue in June 1692 put these plans on indefinite hold. Nevertheless, in the minds of many within the nervous Protestant elite, the Irish Brigade remained a real threat and there was a constant fear that these invasion plans could be revived at short notice.[10] Hurly's allegations of O'Brien's ongoing involvement in conspiratorial Jacobitism chimed well with such fears. Notwithstanding serious doubts in the higher echelons of the administration in respect of the source and validity of such claims, they were sufficiently credible to force the hand of the lords justices to support their detailed investigation in the months leading up to Hurly's trial.

CONTROLLING THE COURTS

Even before what contemporaries referred to as 'the breach at the Boyne' on 1 July 1690 (old style) the Williamite authorities sought to establish control of the Irish court system. A first step was the appointment of Sir Richard Ryves (1643–93), Richard Pyne (1644–1709) and Robert Rochfort as judges of oyer and terminer (local assize courts). All of these new judges were Irish-born senior barristers intimately familiar with local conditions. Pyne and Rochfort were later central players in the Hurly case. Quickly establishing full control of the judicial system at a national and a local level, with its sprawling and nationwide facilitating infrastructure of JPs, constables, county gaols and grand juries, was an immediate requirement enabling the enforcement of the edicts of the new regime, the pursuit of their Jacobite enemies and the restoration/maintenance of local law and order so that the benefits of victory could be more readily enjoyed by the gentry families of the Protestant Ascendancy. Irish histography has tended to present the eighteenth-century criminal justice system as both sectarian and oppressive, but recent work by Neal Garnahm on the system, Timothy Watt on popular protest and policing and David Fleming on expressions of disaffection in Gaelic poetry have presented a more nuanced view of the pervasiveness and indeed the effectiveness of this system.[11] The contemporary importance attached to the Hurly case is illustrated by the involvement of no fewer than six MPs; Alan Brodrick, Robert Rochfort, Sir John Meade and Sir William Handcock acted for the prosecution, while Bernard and John Forster acted for the defence. The Hurly case also involved at least six Clare JPs: Dean Neptune Blood, George Hickman, Thomas Hickman, Augustine FitzGerald, James Cusack and Mr Bindon, while numerous constables, gaolers, a troop of dragoons, the Clare grand jury and the twelve men of the king's bench jury were directly involved in the Hurly trial and in the associated searches, investigations and the preparation of legal documentation.[12]

As part of this judicial strategy both during the war and in the immediate aftermath, the Williamite authorities developed numerous lists of Irish Jacobite outlawries and pardons. In 1699, as part of the work of the commission appointed by the English parliament to inquire into the Irish forfeitures, these lists were consolidated and Simms estimated that the final list ran to more than '4,000 distinct names and addresses, together with a number of particulars of occupation and relationships'.[13] Several members of the Hurly family, including Patrick esq., recorded as resident in Dublin, Lt-Col. John Hurly of Limerick, and John Hurley of Moughna, Co. Clare, appeared on this list. Irish Catholics, however, and their exiled brethren, did not have a monopoly on Irish Jacobitism in this period and, while only a handful of leading Protestant gentry or politicians were active Jacobites, the government remained wary of the potential Jacobite threat, especially during periods of heightened tension associated with recent invasion scares. The invasion scares of 1692 and 1695 were therefore the background against which Hurly was afforded a receptive audience for his accusations against O'Brien. While these accusations, as will be seen, rested at least in part on interpersonal rivalry and on the testimony of very disreputable and unreliable, even fictitious witnesses, they were taken seriously in some quarters. As Ó Ciardha has noted, 'the discovery of personal conflicts does not always deprive such testimony of its value in reflecting an atmosphere of sedition from which it derived its credibility'.[14]

SECURING THE LAND

Following the military victory in the war and the establishment of Irish parliament as a process rather than an event, the ultimate economic prize for the re-established Protestant Ascendancy was to confirm in law their ownership of the land of Ireland and to remove the legal basis of challenges to this hegemony that might emanate from the residual members of the Catholic elite. James Bonnell, the Irish accountant-general, perhaps best expressed the seething resentments within some elements of Protestant opinion. In November 1691, just months after the end of hostilities, and over the course of a long letter to Robert Harley, he averred how "tis plain the Irish are in much better condition then we hoped ... Had the Irish bin totally reduced and brought low by the loss of all their estates, this country would have been looked on by the English as a secure place and many would have flocked hither for advantages to be had, which would have greatly increased our numbers'.[15] As far back as 1976, Simms (in his magisterial *The Williamite confiscation in Ireland, 1690–1703*) noted that 'Catholics owned considerably more land both in 1688 and in 1703' than perhaps had been previously thought. His argument was that 'the articles of Limerick and Galway were of much more importance in preserving Catholic property than appears from the published report of the inquiry commissioners'.[16] Not surprisingly, Protestants of all hues were therefore frustrated by even modest successful legal challenges by Catholic landowners. In particular, they decried how experienced and wily Catholic lawyers such as Sir Toby Butler (*c*.1650–1721), Sir Stephen Rice (1637?–1715), Denis Daly (*c*.1638–

1721) and Edmund Malone were active in representing the Catholic landed interest. The result was a world replete with protracted and contested legal claims and of fluctuating fortunes. Some of these tensions came to a head with a direct intervention from London in the form of the Commission of Inquiry into the Forfeited Estates in Ireland, the establishment of the Trustees for the Sale of the Forfeited Estates and the Act of Resumption of 1700. The commissioners 'lost no opportunity to discredit the government's administration of the forfeitures and to paint a lurid picture of neglect, corruption, favouritism and partiality to papists'.[17] The Inquiry of 1699 identified 1,283 claims under the articles of which all but sixteen were allowed. Most of the 167 claimants from Clare were Catholic and they included several O'Briens.[18] The trustees were therefore especially open to accusations of illegality on the part of Catholic and crypto-Catholic landowners and they made numerous and fruitless efforts to obtain convictions against those who had to date escaped outlawry. Hurly's accusation against O'Brien was one of the more notorious cases that came across their desk and not surprisingly it was given, at least in the initial stages, a sympathetic hearing.

2. Guilty as charged? The trial and conviction of Patrick Hurly

WAS HURLY GUILTY AS CHARGED? DID THE EVIDENCE STACK UP?

This chapter reviews the most important evidence as presented by the prosecution and the defence and as recorded in the *Tryal* and supported by the corroborative detail on the behind-the-scenes activity as extracted from the Inchiquin Papers and state papers. Shortly after the conclusion of the trial, two editions of the *Tryal* pamphlet were published; one in Dublin and another in London.[1] Neither contained any paratexts such as preface, introduction or background details; however, it would seem the reader is expected to believe the text is a verbatim transcript of the lengthy, complex and on occasion opaque evidence presented at the trial. Over the course of a single day, testimony had been heard from a total of twenty-nine sworn witnesses. They included law officers such as Dean Neptune Blood, the JP who had taken Hurly's initial affidavit, several of Hurly's servants, his alleged confederates, a Dublin alderman, three monoglot Irish speakers and a Dublin shopkeeper. Unsurprisingly, there was a wide, and in the final analysis, irreconcilable divergence between the arguments advanced by, and the facts presented by, the prosecution witnesses and the alternative argument and facts as advanced by the witnesses for the defence. While the existence of a background dispute between Hurly and O'Brien was referenced on several occasions during the testimony, it was not a central theme of the prosecution case and there was no reference to the parallel legal process for the investigation of Hurly's allegations of treason against O'Brien.

In his affidavit of 6 March 1700 Hurly described the events of the late evening of Sunday 3 March 1700 in dramatic and colourful detail. He recounted how, at about 11p.m., just as the household was getting ready to bed down for the evening, four or more men, heavily armed with swords and pistols, clad in greatcoats and with their faces hidden by masks broke into his father's house and how they had ransacked the place and stolen coins, jewellery and clothing to the very considerable total value of £1,300. The goods reported as stolen consisted of '374 guineas, and 345 pistoles, a gold cross set with diamonds, and several other diamonds to a great value; and a great number of Holland sheets and Holland shirts'. In his affidavit Hurly estimated that the coins were valued at £848 9s., he valued the jewellery at £225 and the linen at £229; a total of £1,302 9s. He recounted how the robbers swore and shouted calling him a 'rogue, rascal, son of a whore, treacherous villain to his country', how they had fired several shots, how they had threatened and imprisoned his servants, and how he and his visitor Mr Ronane were tied to the bedpost in his bed chamber, before the robbers made good their escape. Hurly further asserted that he did not know any of his assailants but he claimed that 'by the tone of their voice he believed to be Irish-men and papists'. He further indicated his intention to seek compensation for his losses from the taxpayers of Clare under the provisions of the Act for the Better Suppressing Tories, Robbers, Rapparees &c. that had been passed by the Irish parliament in 1695 and amended in 1697. Even at this early stage in the process, and while he was still in the process of making his initial affidavit, Hurly was challenged by Dean Blood as to whether he or others were involved in the robbery so as to seek compensation, to which assertion he declared 'that it was not nor does he know of any such contrivance or design, by any persons whatsoever, either directly or indirectly'.

Within days the authorities both locally in Clare and then in Dublin were convinced that the robbery was nothing more than a sham. By the end of March 1700 Hurly had been arrested and the authorities began the detailed and complex process of compiling the evidence against him. The trial took place fifteen months later at the court of king's bench in Dublin on Saturday 31 May 1701 at the then recently renovated four courts building in Christ Church Yard between Christ Church Cathedral and Skinner's Row.[2] Following a deliberation of only half an hour, the jury found Hurly guilty on both counts. The presiding judge proclaimed: 'as to the perjury, the judgment of the court upon that conviction is, that Mr *Hurly* be fined for the perjury 100*l*. and be imprisoned till he pay it to the king'. The sentence for the attempted 'cheat' was held over until the next court sitting and it is not recorded either in the trial transcript or in any of the other sources used in this book. It would seem that Hurly never paid the fine. Two years later in June 1703 Edward Southwell (1671–1730), chief secretary for Ireland, writing from Dublin to Daniel Finch, 2nd earl of Nottingham (1647–1730), secretary of state in London, noted that 'it will with submission be proper to have Hurly taken up, for he is certainly a very great rogue & has broke gaol here in the queens debt upon a fin: so that were he here or sent over, wee have enough against him'. The involvement of Hurly in what appears to be an ill-conceived and poorly planned attempt on the life of Queen Anne raises the interesting, if perhaps unlikely, further possibility that Hurly was a genuine Jacobite patriot with an enduring commitment to the cause.

THE SCENE OF THE CRIME; THE HURLY FARMHOUSE IN MOUGHNA

The robbery at the centre of this book is said to have taken place on the evening of Sunday 3 March 1700. In most contemporary records, following the so-called old-style dating conventions, this date was written as 3 March 1699, and consequently in some of the historiography the incident has been ascribed incorrectly to 1699 instead of 1700. The location of the robbery was the farmhouse of John Hurly, Patrick Hurly's elderly and bed-ridden father, in the townland of Moughna in north-central Co. Clare. While the farmhouse was not a grand house, let alone a 'big' house, it must have been one of considerable size. Witnesses in the trial referenced numerous rooms including a kitchen, a parlour, several bed chambers, as well as outhouses. They also referred to a series of new walls that had been constructed by Hurly in the months before the robbery as the house became the 'garrison'. The house was sufficiently large to have accommodated up to thirteen people on the evening of the robbery. While the Hurlys do not appear to have been particularly rich, it was clear that they employed a retinue of farm hands and servants and undoubtedly they would have had some considerable status in the local community. The Hurlys could perhaps be considered as an early example of what Kevin Whelan called the 'underground gentry'.[3] In the eighteenth century the most usual spelling of the townland was Moughna, and this spelling is used throughout this book. The Irish name is *Múchna*, which means 'darkness' or 'gloom', apparently because the townland lies under the shadow of nearby Mount Callan.[4] Viscount Mountcallan was one of the many aliases used by Hurly. The townland consists of *c*.280 hectares or 700 acres, and it is in the electoral division of Magherareagh, in the civil parish of Clooney and the barony of Corcomroe. Moughna is located approximately 24km (15 miles) from the county town of Ennis and 6.3km (4 miles) from Ennistymon. It is a remote place and somewhat off the beaten track; as local historian Colm Liddy put it on Clare FM in 2023, 'You wouldn't go there unless you meant to; it's not on the road to anywhere'.[5] In 1641 the townland of Moughna was recorded as being in the ownership of Dermot O'Bryan, a Catholic. By 1670 it was recorded as being in the possession of Thomas Butler, the earl of Ossory, a Protestant.[6] The townland of Moughna includes a graveyard with a holy well, Tobarmooghan. For decades after the War of Independence the townland contained the grave of George Chalmers, a young British army soldier who was captured and killed by the local IRA. In 2018 his remains were exhumed and reinterred in the British army graveyard on Blackhorse Avenue in Dublin.[7]

THE PROSECUTION CASE

The trial commenced with 'The prisoner being brought from the Marshalsea to the bar'. Hurly had been in custody in Ennis from the end of March 1700, a warrant for his arrest having been issued by Thomas Hickman and Augustine FitzGerald, two Clare JPs on 25 March 1700, only three weeks after the alleged robbery. According to the evidence of a Richard Roch and recorded in the state papers, Hurly had been transferred to the Marshalsea in Dublin sometime in June. Following some challenges by the prisoner, the details of which were not specified in the *Tryal* text, the jury of twelve men were sworn in. The jurors were Edmund Perry, James McDonnel, John Brady, Denis MacMahon, Richard Henn, Thomas Brown, John Drew, Hugh Brady, Edward Mealing, Austin Bennis, Joseph Cecil and Patrick Connell. These were all men from Clare; a detail that was not mentioned in the *Tryal* text but which was highlighted by Hurly in *Innocence Justify'd* where he called them 'the resolute twelve' who had brought in their 'premeditated verdict'. He also alleged that Drew had told him 'there was not above three or four of the impannel'd durst have return'd to the county of Clare, if they had not brought in their verdict against me'. From a very early date Hurly had tried to avoid being tried by a Clare jury. On 29 March he had written to the clerk of the king's bench court in Dublin looking to have a *habeas corpus* sent to Clare so that he could be transferred to Dublin where he might face a 'Protestant jury'. In line with contemporary practice, all the jurors were men of some standing in their community and it is almost certain that all were Protestants. Four of the jurors – Edmund Perry, Richard Henn, Patrick Connell and Thomas Brown – were listed among the 167 from Clare who made claims to the Trustees for Forfeited Estates at Chichester House in 1700.[8] Other Clare men who featured on these lists, and who were involved in, or who were mentioned during, the Hurly case, included James McDonnel, Neptune Blood, Donat O'Brien, Henry Hickman, Francis Burton, Theobald Butler and Lord Clare.

The formal proceedings got underway when the clerk of the court recited the charges. The first charge was

> that Patrick Hurly stands here, indicted of perjury; for swearing before Neptune Blood dean of Kilfenora, one of his majesties justices of the peace for the county of Clare that he was Robbed of three hundred pistoles in gold, and several other things, by four persons altogether unknown to him but whom by the tone of their voice he believed to be Irishmen and Papists, whereas in truth and fact he well knew them by the names and persons, being sett on by himself, and did not take anything at all from him.

The second charge was that 'the same Patrick Hurly stands here indicted, for that he did falsely and deceitfully conspire with one Daniel Hickey and several other malefactors, unjustly to oppress the popish inhabitants of the country of Clare and cheat them of a great sum of money, by colour of the Rapparee Act'. The prosecution case was then opened by statements from the two most senior law officers – the attorney general Alan Brodrick and the solicitor general Robert

Rochfort. They commenced by putting the full text of Hurly's affidavit of 6 March into the official court record. The prosecution case was that the robbery was 'All false, and nothing in it, but a mock robbery, acted by persons imployed and set on by himself'. Logically, therefore, they asserted that if the perjury was proven then 'The second is the consequence of the first. If Mr Hurly was really truly robbed, then he did not design to cheat the country'.[9] The core prosecution contention was that the motivation for the sham robbery was that Hurly 'instead of being a man of so much cash at that time, was the contrary to an extream degree'. They also contended that in the months before the alleged robbery Hurly had boasted that 'by the act of parliament, if he could fix a robbery on the country, he could tax what sum he pleased'. To further corroborate their argument that the entire escapade was fraudulent, the prosecution also claimed that they would produce witnesses to prove that 'the gold he pretended to lose was but counters'. The prosecution's main witness was Calaghan Carty, one of Hurly's servants and one of four suspects arrested for the robbery. Carty confirmed many of the details of Hurly's version of events such as the red coats and the 'vizards' (defined by Johnson as a mask used for disguise) worn by the robbers. He related how Hurly had shown him a purse of gold that he needed to pay a debt to a Mr Arthur who was due to 'compound with him' and of Hurly's subsequent declaration that if he gave Arthur the money he would be 'ruin'd for ever'. He testified that Hurly claimed that 'if Mr Arthur should hear the money was robbed, he would compound with him'. The inference was that in these changed circumstances Arthur would cut Hurly some slack. Carty named the other participants in the robbery as Donough O'Brien Andrews, Daniel Hickey (Hurly's brother-in-law), Daniel Carty and Teige Carty; three of whom were described in later testimony as Hurly's servants. When questioned about the weapons used in the robbery, Carty claimed that the swords had been brought from Dublin by Hurly, and provided to the robbers by Daniel MacCaie, Hurly's footman and his alleged principal collaborator in the implementation of the 'sham robbery'. He recounted how several firearms had been left on a table by MacCaie, and that they were charged with powder. He further asserted that in the weeks prior to the robbery Hurly's house had become something of a 'garrison' with some servants always on alert as Hurly 'was on his keeping, for fear of being taken upon writs and executions, he had servants in his house, and he kept one watching constantly for fear of being taken'.[10] He confirmed that the creditor in question was the aforementioned Mr Arthur. The almost casual reference to the regular presence of guns and swords in the house of a well-known Catholic with Jacobite sympathies, a fact that was unlikely to have gone unnoticed by the local JPs, is interesting at a time when the strictures against the right of Catholics to bear arms was an integral and important part of the state's security policy. In a letter dated 5 October 1699 and cited later in the trial, Hurly casually referenced how he had 'detached Corporal Malone, for ammunition' and how he asked Capt. MacDonogh to 'send me a pound of the best powder, and three dozen of carbine musket and pistol ball'. Hurly was not listed as a Catholic allowed to possess arms.

As the trial progressed it became clear, both from the attention paid to the point by the prosecution witnesses and from the answers given in response to several interjections by Hurly and members of his defence team, that a key point of Hurly's counter-argument was that, while the four accused were in gaol in Ennis, they had been threatened with hanging – 'you shall stretch for it' – and that they had only made the statements implicating themselves in the 'sham robbery' under duress. Hurly and his barrister further claimed that on their release the four had gone to Dublin and signed retractions in front of Chief Justice Pyne. Very early in the proceedings, Rochfort sought to rebut this assertion when he declared 'My lord, Mr Hurly pretends that this man [Calaghan Carty] gave an examination contrary to this. Now we will shew you that that was done by another person, empoly'd by Mr Hurly to personate this man'. The judge challenged Rochfort: 'do you admit that there was an examination?' (a statement before Justice Pyne), to which Rochfort replied 'there was an examination sworn before my lord chief justice ... but this was not the man'. When Carty was asked 'was you sworn before my lord Chief Justice Pyne?', he replied 'never in my life' and he claimed that the signature on the examination was 'none of my hand'. The prosecution left it to the judge and jury to draw their own conclusion. Pyne was not called to give evidence. Later in the trial his clerk was called to testify but he claimed that as he was 'busie' and when these statements were sworn, he could not identify those who had been present.

One curious feature of the *Tryal* text, and of the Inchiquin Papers, is the almost complete absence of Ronane, Hurly's visitor on the night of the robbery and who allegedly had been tied up along with Hurly by the raiders. Ronane was not called as a witness at the trial and although a later witness John Hurly (Patrick's brother) later claimed that he and his servant had been examined by the JPs shortly after the robbery although no statement or affidavit was submitted in evidence. The Inchiquin Papers contain a copy of a statement from John Ronane of 'Glenstale, Co. Limerick', dated 4 March 1700, in which he repeated the standard narrative of how the raiders had burst into the house and fired several shots. When asked by the defence lawyers whether Ronane 'was privy at all this robbery?', Carty replied 'I don't know; I believe he may for I know no other business he had there, nor I saw no other business he did there'. Later in the trial, Dorothy Kemp, a key witness for the defence, claimed that Ronane had been there for three days 'waiting for Mr Arthur to pay him some money'. The only other substantive reference to Ronane in the *Tryal* is the testimony from several witnesses that the raid had commenced when Ronane had 'gone abroad' (i.e., outdoors), presumably to go to the outhouse; and that his going out was the occasion for the raiders to storm the house. Ronane's absence seems strange. All of the other eyewitnesses to the events in the farmhouse in Moughna on the night of the robbery, including the four accused robbers, were either servants or relatives of Hurly. While Ronane clearly had some business connection with Hurly, he or his manservant who was also present in the house that evening, might have been able to provide at least a modicum of third-party evidence for these events. In 1711 a John Ronan esq. of Limerick, possibly the same person, was recorded in the Registry of Deeds as being an arbitrator in a debt dispute; so he does not appear to have died in the meantime.[11]

Over the course of the day, the prosecution called a series of witnesses and continued to build its case. One of the most important was Margaret Coneene, a servant in Hurly's house and a monoglot Irish speaker, known to the family as Peggy Rabbet. The etymology of the Irish and English names was explained to the court. During the trial an unnamed interpreter, presumably male, was sworn in and interpreted for three witnesses – Margaret Coneene, Mortogh MacCollogy (a neighbour of the Hickeys) and John Crips, a Hurly tenant. The text of the *Tryal* made no mention of the interpreter's competence or qualification or of any payment. There is no hint, however, that there was any issue with their competence.[12] Coneene testified that 'at first she was of opinion that it was a real robbery' but now 'she was of another opinion'. She claimed that this was upon the account of 'a table cloth taken away at the time of the robbery, which she saw afterwards come back in a trunk or portmanteau that was sent to Mr O'Brien after the robbery'. She also testified, as an aside, that Carty had been arrested with the support of 'some dragoons'. She confirmed that some shots had been fired but that 'they hurt no body, and they saw no holes or marks of shots or bullets'. She further testified that there were always some firearms in the house, that they belonged to Mr Hurly, and that they were usually on the table in the parlour and not stored away. She knew of 'a couple of fuzees, a blunderbuss, a couple of carbines and pistols'. During her testimony, she averred how the robbers had locked the door and that they had left the arms outside, at which point the solicitor general could not help but exclaim 'upon my word a man that had robbed 1300*l*. would hardly have parted with his arms till he was safe lodged'. She concluded by saying that she saw the arms in the house again shortly afterwards.

The challenge to her evidence centred not on her testimony in respect of the arms, or of the return of the stolen goods, but rather on the issue of her service/employment in the period since the robbery; the implication being that she had been suborned or threatened for her testimony. It was during this examination – one of the few occasions on which the questioning approximated modern cross-examination practice – that the name of Sir Donat O'Brien was first mentioned by a witness. In a series of somewhat opaque answers, she said that she had gone to O'Brien's house 'to give an account of what she knew concerning this robbery', but she did not speak with O'Brien, rather gave a statement to a justice of the peace, whose name she did not know. In a further series of questions, she claimed that she was not 'tampered with' in any way or offered any promise of 'a portion'. When she was asked if she 'did not hear the country and all the neighbourhood say that if they did not make this no robbery, Sir Donagh would be ruin'd', she said 'she heard no such thing'. As already noted, the theme of suborning and threatening witnesses was a running thread of witness testimonies, and it was a central plank of the defence position. For example, a Walter Neylan who was in Ennis Gaol for debts due to Hurly, and who for a time was lodged in the same room as Hurly, related his understanding as to how the accused came to make their statements. Neylan was almost certainly a relative of O'Brien as Donat's mother's first husband was Daniel Neylan.[13] He claimed that within a few days of their being arrested, three of the alleged robbers had 'discover'd the robbery, and that the other held out for two or three days'. He related how the last prisoner Donough O'Brien Andrews had told him that Hurly needed to 'take care for my releasement, or else I must discover as well as the rest'. Neylan then related how Hurly had asked him to bribe Andrews, claiming that Hurly feared the testimony of his servants because they were fully aware of the contrivance.

There seems to be little doubt that in the spring of 1700 Hurly was in dire financial straits and the prosecution sought to make the most of this point. In January 1701 as part of his information gathering, O'Brien had sourced a certificate from the marshal of the four courts of outstanding 'executions and actions' for debt against Hurly; they amounted to £775 17s. 2d. and his creditors included Thomas Arthur (figs 3, 4). In no instance in the trial text or in the Inchiquin Papers was the business underlying these sizable financial transactions specified. Hurly admitted that he owed Arthur £723 and confirmed that he had sought the help of Sir Toby Butler to reach an accommodation with Arthur. It is not clear whether Hurly would have been aware that Butler was also an advisor to and in the end a supporter of O'Brien. Capt. Charles MacDonogh, Hurly's solicitor, claimed that while he was 'employ'd by him (i.e., Hurly) in negotiating several affairs in the country, and particularly against his brother, that ow'd him some money' and that 'I thought he was severe against his brother, and I charg'd him for being so unkind to him'. In a letter dated 5 October 1699 (before the robbery), which was read out in court and which the prosecution presented as proof of his financial distress, Hurly recounted how he expected to be 'blocked up very soon, or rather regularly besieged by the formidable Capt. Thomas Bourk, and select party he brags to have hired of the Enniskillin Dragoons for that purpose'. Prosecution witnesses also claimed that the Christmas before the robbery Hurly had claimed to McDonagh that the 'Rapparee Act was a clever way to recover money from the country'.

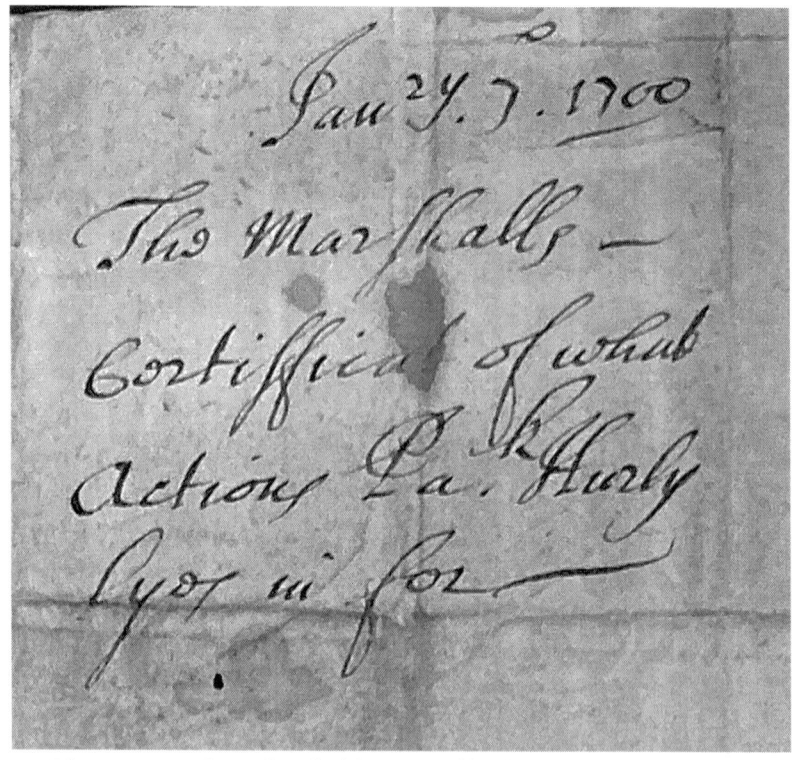

3. File note on certificate of Hurly debts prepared by the marshal of the Four Courts, 9 Jan. 1700/1 (source: NLI Inchiquin Papers MS 45,330/4)

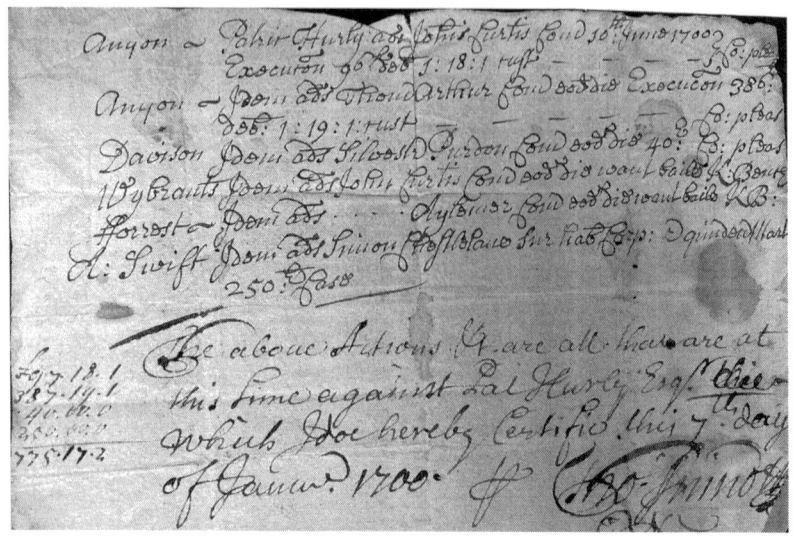

4. Certificate of Hurly debts prepared by the marshal of the Four Courts, 9 Jan. 1700/1 (source: NLI Inchiquin Papers MS 45,330/4)

A further central plank of the prosecution case was that the 'stolen' gold coins that had been so conspicuously seen by many witnesses in the weeks leading up to the robbery were in fact mere 'counters'. One witness, Mortagh MacCologhy, mentioned that when he was offered some of these counters by Daniel Hickey's wife (Hurly's sister) in payment for a cow he knew they 'were some of Patrick's Hurly's gold'. The implication was that this was common local knowledge. He also claimed that, at the suggestion of Donat O'Brien, he had shown the coins to Mr Bindon, a local JP. Unfortunately, a feature of the evidence as recorded in the *Tryal* text is a lack of exactitude in respect of dates and on the exact sequence of events. In this instance MacCologhy stated this had occurred 'around Christmas 1700'. He further asserted that in February 1701 Daniel Hickey's wife had claimed that she had retained some of the counters and that she would produce them in court as evidence. MacCologhy then reported this to Mr Butler JP and on foot of this intelligence searches were organized, first of Hurly's father's house, then of the nearby Carty house, and finally of Hickey's house. The tale of their discovery in a dunghill beside Hickey's house was recounted in court in an almost comic rendition of how the search party were asked not to dig in an area which clearly showed evidence of fresh digging and where Mrs Hickey claimed she had recently stored some potatoes. Not surprisingly, this testimony was rejected by Hurly who claimed that it was a set-up and that the coins/counters had been planted by O'Brien's agents; as Bernard his defence counsel put it, 'the man that found them, hid them'.

The final important testimony presented by the prosecution was that of Capt. Lynch, the Hurlys' long-time landlord: 'he and his father was tenants to me and my father these forty years'. In fact, he had a much more complex and close relationship with the Hurlys as his sister was married to Hurly's brother. In his testimony, Lynch hinted, without giving detail, that there was a simmering land dispute between himself and Hurly's father. Lynch also shed light on the relations between Hurly and O'Brien, claiming that Hurly said that 'Sir Donogh O'Brien was the greatest enemy he had against him, ... but he would lose his blood, or he should lose his'. Reflecting the close interconnection between the parties, he also provided evidence for the early ideation of making a claim under the terms of the rapparee acts. Lynch further claimed that in the course of their conversation Hurly had enquired as to how Banks's money went. This was a reference to a claim made by Banks who had been robbed of £250 and how 'the grand jury, at the assizes, allow'd him the money when he petition'd for it'. In the same conversation he claimed that Hurly had asked for Lynch's help in organizing events so that he could make such a claim; Lynch claimed that he demurred, saying 'I would assist him in any just way, but no further'. Later Hurly not totally unreasonably claimed in *Innocence Justify'd* that given how he was in the middle of a major dispute with Lynch he would be very unlikely to turn to him for support. In the course of his testimony, Lynch added a further unsolicited hearsay comment that about a year earlier 'Richard Hurly, Patrick's uncle declar'd to me, that it was a sham robbery'.

THE CASE FOR THE DEFENCE

The case for defence, or the traverser (the term used in the *Tryal* text), was opened by Hurly's leading defence lawyer Francis Bernard, the Cork-born MP and leading Tory. Barnard argued that most, if not all, of the evidence adduced by the state had been secured by suborning and threatening witnesses. He grandiosely opened his argument by declaiming 'If your lordships will hear the proofs, we shall turn the table'. He claimed that he could show that 'Mr Hurly was a man that came with a good fund of money into this kingdom and left a good fund in France'. He claimed that Arthur had nefariously intervened to prevent Hurly from repatriating those funds. He alluded to the 'quarrel between Mr Hurly and Sir Donagh O'Brien' and noted that 'Sir Donagh had such great interest in the country, prevailed with the jury for some reasons, that the presentment was not found for us at the assizes' (i.e., Hurly's compensation claim at the Ennis assizes), which prevented Hurly from gaining the money owed by him to Arthur. He described how the four men who had been 'taken up for the robbery, and laid in irons' were threatened 'here is life or death proposed, if you confess the matter and place it upon Hurly, you shall have your lives, but if you do not, as soon as the commission comes down you shall stretch for it'. He concluded by relating how these alleged robbers had gone to Lord Justice Pyne to retract their earlier statements, how Hicky's wife had hidden the counters 'where it may be found' and that 'these prosecutions have been carried on by bribery, and such like practices'.

The defence case got off to a poor start when their first witness Charles FitzSimons, a Dublin merchant, was called but did not appear; he was to give evidence of the significant sums that had gone through Hurly's hands in the last years of the century. In a lengthy testimony, John Hurly, Patrick's brother who was in gaol on foot of an execution for debt from Patrick, sought to show the scale of his brother's financial means by recounting how, as a receiver for his brother, he had transacted £400 with Col. Lovet and £306 with FitzSimons. He also confirmed the presence of the gold in the house prior to the robbery, which he said Hurly's wife had told him was 'to pay off Arthur'. He also shone further light on the dispute between their landlord and his father when he claimed that Lynch had disposed of the reversion of the lease over the head of the sitting tenant. In addition, he claimed to have seen, but he did not produce a copy of, a note that had been given to Hickey by two Clare JPs, Hickman and Cusack, promising 'to intercede with the government for pardon, for him and others, if they proved the robbery on Patrick Hurly'. John Hurly also admitted that he had been in custody since April for debts due to his brother and on foot of claims by other creditors including the aforementioned FitzSimons who had claimed that Patrick had not paid him the money due and which John said he had collected and paid over to his brother. Perhaps the most important defence witness was Dorothy Kemp, a servant of Hurly's wife. During her testimony, which was given via an interpreter, she referred to the robbers as 'Tories', a term that was used on only one other occasion during the trial by the judge in his summing up. During Kemp's testimony she claimed that Murrough O'Brien had offered her a bribe of £10 to hide the counters in either Hurly's or Hicky's house. When Murrough O'Brien was duly called and sworn and asked 'had you any discourse with this woman concerning counters?', he declared 'I never had', to which Kemp replied 'by virtue of my oath, you did'. There followed one of only a handful of what could be termed short-tempered spats, between either the legal teams, the judge or a witness or, on this occasion, between witnesses. Murrough O'Brien continued 'it's a very improbable thing, if I had a mind to tamper with her, that I would tamper with Hurly's Whore – my lord, if I wou'd have come on such a business, would any one believe that I should employ this woman that has had a bastard or two by Mr Hurley'. This personal piece of character assassination was apparently not challenged by either the court or the defence team. Later, when Kemp repeated some further hearsay evidence from Mrs Hurly, Mr Foster, one of the defence lawyers, remarked that 'we only offer it as far as it will go', to which the attorney general replied tersely 'It will not go at all'. The judge made no comment.

As in many court cases, some of the testimony seemed to do more harm than good. In a lengthy, tetchy and almost incomprehensible testimony from Hurly's footman Daniel McCay, in respect of the route taken while he was returning with Hurly to Clare from Dublin some months before the robbery, he was decidedly unclear as to how they had crossed the Shannon. When asked sharply, and presumably somewhat tongue in cheek, 'did you swim over, or go over a bridge?', he meekly replied 'I think we went over a bridge'. He did support the suborning argument when he testified that 'I was offer'd to have my fortune raised for ever if I would swear, that he bought the counters, and brought them to the county of Clare' although he then claimed that he was sure that the coins he had seen in Dublin sometime earlier were gold, noting that 'it was Louis d'ores'. The defence case continued when Crips, a tenant of Hurly's, the third monoglot Irish speaker, also testified that he had been offered both cash and grazing rights by Christopher O'Brien if he would testify against Hurly. At this point one of the prosecution lawyers intervened to declare 'My lord, this man does not seem to be a man of any credit'. Following this, Judge Coote noted 'if two witnesses speak directly contrary one to the other, must not it be left to the jury which they will believe?' Lynch and Neylan then disputed aspects of Crips's testimony. Lynch swore that he had not made any offer to Crips and Neylan swore that he never 'saw the man, till this day, never since he was born'. Christopher O'Brien also denied that he had made any such offer. Crips reported that the dispute between the Hurlys and their landlord Lynch had reached a point where he reported Lynch as saying 'they are both in irons, and they never retrieve it' and 'I have set the land from the Hurlys to the Bloods and Hurly shall never have anything to say to it more'. In the absence of clear evidence, it is difficult to disentangle the complex business and land-leasing arrangements between the leading figures in Clare society. What is clear is that Neptune Blood was an active participant in the land market in Clare; for example, a decade later in 1710 he signed a complex lease for three lives for ninety-six acres from O'Brien.[14]

The defence case concluded with several of the alleged robbers taking the stand and repeating the narrative of the threats of being hanged that had been made against the four accused by the local JPs Hickman, Butler and Cusack and how, following changing their testimony, they and Crips 'came to town and made an affidavit before him' (Justice Pyne, lord chief justice).

GATHERING THE EVIDENCE

In the fifteen months between the alleged robbery in early March 1700 and the trial at the end of May 1701 all parties to the case (Hurly, O'Brien and the authorities in Clare, Dublin Castle and London) had been active in gathering evidence to support their case. The largest corpus for these behind-the-scenes activities is the (no doubt incomplete but nevertheless extensive) archive of over three hundred letters, copies of legal documents, legal briefs and other papers compiled by O'Brien. It is not clear how he constructed the file, but it is possible that some papers were provided to him by sympathetic officials or by members of the prosecution team. It is also not clear when O'Brien came into possession of these documents and therefore it is hard to judge how much was known to the prosecution team at the time of the trial. The Inchiquin archive also clearly demonstrates that O'Brien, his son Lucius, his sister and no doubt many of his Protestant, convert and Catholic friends such as Sir Humphry Jervis and Sir Toby Butler had been engaged in a letter-writing and evidence-gathering campaign on his behalf. O'Brien claimed that, despite Hurly having been active as Jacobite official in the Clare, Limerick and Galway region during the latter stages of the war, and that his father had rented a farm in the mid-Clare area where O'Brien had extensive holdings for forty years, his first interaction with Hurly had occurred only in early 1698. This contention is supported by a letter dated 5 February 1698 in which Hurly acknowledged O'Brien's support in his efforts to recover a coin hoard that Hurly had purportedly buried on land leased by O'Brien prior to his departure for France after the surrender of Limerick. Whatever its origins, the tension between O'Brien, or at least some members of his family, and Hurly pre-dated the robbery of March 1700. For example, in January 1700 O'Brien's cousin Timothy related how he had heard (incorrectly, it would appear) that Hurly qualified under the articles of Limerick and how he had gone to Dublin to obtain a reversal of his outlawry after which 'hee desinges to fall on mee, and turn mee out of my farm'. The farm in question was leased from Lord Ikerrin. Timothy had looked to O'Brien for support.

The evidence in the Inchiquin file also shows that the authorities were convinced of the sham-robbery hypothesis from a very early date. As early as 27 March 1700 the local JPs Thomas Hickman and Joseph Cusack had arranged to meet O'Brien to brief him on the sham robbery and on 30 March Thomas Hickman wrote to Sir John Hely, the lord chief justice, requesting a commission to come to Ennis to try Hurly for the robbery which had been 'detected as a contrivance of his owne'. Intelligence on Hurly's intention to drag O'Brien into the courts on foot of his accusations of treason and the accusation that O'Brien was behind the robbery can be traced to an early date. On 6 April Neylan reported to O'Brien that Hurly had written to Lord Galway and Rochfort of what Hurly termed the

> pretended Protestants but inward Jacobits of the county of Clare & particularly Sir Donatt o Brien who is the lead card of the sd county, are plotting and contriving all the ways their witts can suggest to doe him prejudice; and that latelie to accomplish their malitious intents, as well as to hinder him from doieng his Majestie considerable services which they knew he was a doing) they imployd (as he has reason to believe) some 9 or 10 persons of the county to robb his house; and were not content to refuse him justice according to law &c but gott the sd persons to sweare it was by his own consent & will whereupon he was taken & kept in Irons; he desires ye Attorney Genll may send him down a *noli presequi & a certioriari*. It was my knowledge of this that occasioned the letter to be intercepted.

The trial and conviction of Patrick Hurly

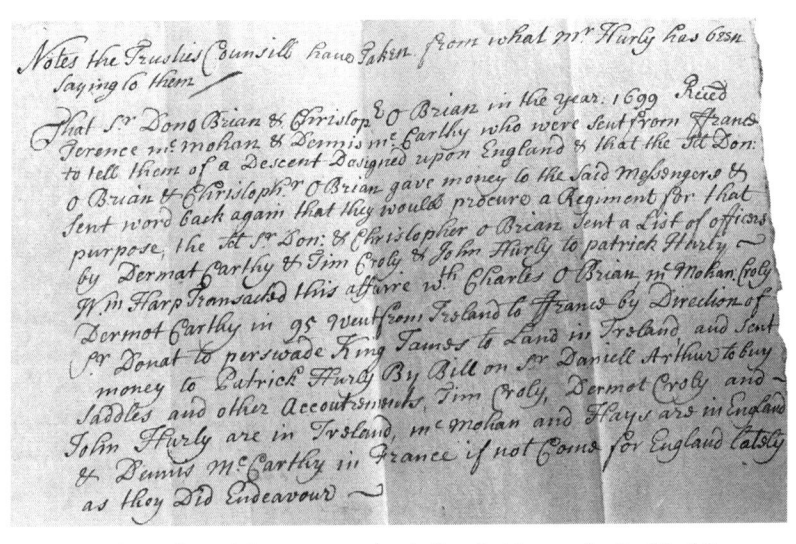

5. Note of Patrick Hurly's testimony taken before the Trustees for Forfeited Estates, June 1700 (source: NLI Inchiquin Papers MS 45,335/2)

It is also clear from the file that the legal officers involved in this case, and indeed a wider cohort of senior officials in Dublin and in London, were unimpressed by Hurly's allegations, being fully convinced of Hurly's ill-character and reputation (fig. 5). They also came to the view that the witnesses Hurly claimed he would be able to bring from France were but a chimera. Nevertheless, the accusations had gained some traction and by end of November Lucius expressed the view to his father that 'it is the positive opinion of every friend he has that his presence in Dublin is absolutely necessary'. Furthermore, by this time Hurly's accusations had achieved sufficient traction in the public sphere that on 17 December the London newspaper *The Flying post; or, The Postmaster* reported that 'Sir Donnagh O Bryan Knight and Bar. was committed by the Government for High Treason, as being commissioned in the late King's Service, and not having reversed his Outlawry'. The following edition of the same paper reported that 'Sir Donah O-Brian, mention'd in my last is admitted to Bail, his Accusers Reputation not being extraordinary'.[15]

Just as O'Brien was not a passive observer of events, Hurly also sought to manage the flow of information to his advantage. In a letter to Thomas Hewlet, dated 29 March 1700, he claimed 'noe man in the world meet wth such a fatall stroak of misfortune as I did ... eleaven person who came in arm'd or mask'd into my house the 3d instant to robb me'. It might be the case that this and other letters were simply tactics by Hurly aimed at creating an evidential paper trail confirming his view of events that might to be of use later. On the same day, writing from the gaol in Ennis and just three days after his confinement, Hurly requested Daniel Wybrants, a court official in Dublin, to seek a *habeus corpus* order to have him moved to Dublin for the trial to take place in front of a Protestant jury. Hurly's specific accusation against O'Brien was that he had first-hand evidence not just that O'Brien was a Jacobite sympathizer but that he had been and continued to be an active conspirator and supporter of Jacobite cause in the years after the conclusion of hostilities. Hurly claimed that while he was in France he had provided advice to King James on individuals that might be of service in the Muster/Clare area and how some of those were sent to Ireland to gather intelligence and to garner support for the cause. Specifically, he claimed that

> this informant further deponeth, that he this Informt then saw at La Hogue aforesaid, letters which the said McCarthy & McMahon brought to Coll. Charles O'Brien & Capt. Randle McDonnell from Sir Donogh, als Sr Donat O'Brien of the county of Clare Barrt. together with a bill of £400 sterl. which the said Sr Donogh said in his letter were to be laid out for arms & furniture for horse, and this inform^t verily believes & is satisfied the said letters were writ by the said Sr Donogh O'Brien, and further, that he this infomrnt does not doubt to prove by several credible persons, that the said Sr Donogh & Capt. Christ. O'Brien encouraged & advised the landing of troopes and levying a warr against the present king and government, at a time when he the said Sr Donogh was a parliament man here. That is to say in the years 1692 and 1695, when the late King James was at Calices & La Hogue in ffrance with an army to invade England.

By December O'Brien's case had come before the lords justices and in due course the Privy Council. On 7 December the lords justices provided a report of over twenty pages, for James Vernon, secretary of state in London. This report included depositions from Hurly and his main co-accusers, Turlough MacMahon and Charles McCarthy. These depositions not only detailed O'Brien's purported treasonous actions during the war of 1689–91 but more importantly it accused him of active Jacobitism during the invasion scares of 1692 and 1695. The accusations were sufficiently grave that the lords justices dispatched a senior judge, Thomas Coote, and the solicitor general, Alan Brodrick (both of whom were to feature some months later in the perjury trial), to examine Hurly. When the judge wanted to meet with Hurly and his co-accusers, however, he was 'by letter acquainted him that they were gone into England ... by reason they expected no success with the Irish juries in their prosecution of Sir Donogh O'Brien'. Hurly then offered to use the good offices of his brother in London to make them available to the law officers. He took care to advise his co-accusers to go into hiding in order to avoid the authorities, who might want to transfer them to Ireland, and to avoid what he termed 'Sir Donat's spies'. Simultaneously, the lords justices asked Vernon to ensure 'that they may have such protections or licences forthwith despatched, as may be necessary to leave them without excuse for not repairing hither'. Hurly's witnesses never appeared in either London or Dublin. The matter was then brought before the privy council:

> We laid these examinations before the councill yesterday, for Sr Donogh being a man of very considerable fortune, interest and figure in his countrey, we were willing to advise with them what measures were proper to be taken on this occasion, who were of opinion that the common methode of the law should be pursued, so the examinations were by them put into the hands of the lord chief justice of the king's bench in order to be proceeded upon according to law.

Hurly frequently asserted that he would only submit his evidence and advise his witnesses to appear if the trial took place in England where he felt the law officers and a jury would be beyond the financial interest of O'Brien and his allies. For example on 2 December 1700 he wrote to Justice Thomas Coote reiterating his view that he had no confidence in the Irish justice system and noting that some of his witnesses had returned to England because they believed that nothing would come of their accusations and that without the necessary passes they could be charged and indicted if they returned to Ireland. He concluded with a criticism of the judiciary: 'the constitution of Irish judges are such at present that they will find no indictm't for foreigne treason ... agst any man of fortune or interest but on the contrary the prosecutions are looked upon as odious and scandalous'. He was also aware that O'Brien was maximizing his own sources of intelligence. In the same letter, Hurly claimed that 'there is not a coffee house or tavern in the city but Sir Donogh has a pensioner in it to decry me and to rept.'

The lords justices were equally determined that any trial would be in Ireland: 'inasmuch as we conceive it very materiall for his Maties service and the good of this kingdom that Sir Donogh O'Brien should receive his tryall here in as solemn a manner and as soon as may be. He is, upon some advice of this matter, come up to this towne in order to offer himself to be tryed'. The report concluded with a brief comment in respect of Hurly's character: 'We think it upon this occasion not improper to acquaint you with the character of Patrick Hurly, so farr as the same hath come to our knowledge, he went with the Irish, after the surrender of Limerick, into France and, being there an agent for some of their troopes deserted from them with a summe of money, when the earl of Gallway was in Piedmont, and returned into this kingdome since the conclusion of the Peace at Reswick'. In early December O'Brien made his way to Dublin. A further report to Vernon dated 24 December gave an update on events. It included the text of an examination of O'Brien and a confirmation that Lord Chief Justice Pyne had 'issued his warrant against Sir Donogh, and he was committed to gaol'. The report continued 'where having remained one night, he was next day sett at liberty, having first given very considerable baile before the Lord Chief Justice for his appearance next terme'. As already noted, O'Brien's arrest and release were reported in a London newspaper. In his examination, taken by Pyne and Coote, O'Brien denied almost every point in the Hurly statement. He claimed that he had only become acquainted with Hurly in January 1698. This was clearly at odds with Hurly's declaration to have seen and met with O'Brien in Limerick during the war. O'Brien recounted how in February of the same year he had written to Hurly on behalf of a tenant concerning money that had allegedly been hidden by Hurly prior to his departure to France and which had been found by the sub-tenant who was now unwilling to return it. He also claimed that he 'never drew a bill on Sir Daniel Arthur in Paris' and that he never wrote to Charles O'Brien, 'commonly called Lord Clare'. He concluded by defending his actions during the war, noting that 'he was made sheriff of Co. Clare in 1689 without his knowledge, at the request of the Protestant inhabitants of the said county to the then Mr Justice Daly, judge of assize' and that 'he had no troopes in the late King James his army, but had a guard of about twenty men to preserve the stock of the inhabitants from the Rapparees ... the twenty men so raised were servants to the Protestant inhabitants of the said county'.

HURLY V. O'BRIEN

There does not appear to be any extant image of Hurly and it is unlikely that one was ever made. In 1709 the *London Gazette* described Hurly as being 'about 45 years of age, of a brown complexion, a scar on his forehead, a mole on his cheek, and shot through one of his arms, which arm and hand is bigger that the other, and born in the county of Clare in Ireland'.[16] There is no mention of this injury in the *Tryal* text. In January 1711 another London newspaper reported Hurly as having deserted out of Col. Charteris's foot guards. In this report he was described as 'a insty [sic] fat man, about 45 years of age, 5 foot 10 inches high'.[17] That an excessively fat man could serve as a soldier seems a little improbable, although his role as bursar/agent for the regiment, receiving funds from the treasury and paying soldiers and buying supplies would not have necessitated a battlefield level of fitness. If the age is correct, then Hurly would have been in his mid-30s in 1700 but only in his mid-20s during the war years. In January 1716 Hurly's death was reported in an unusually lengthy entry in the *Dublin Evening Post* (fig. 6):

> Some days ago, Patrick Hurley, the notorious cheat (who came into this kingdom about four months since, and to this city about five weeks ago) took lodgings near St Mary's Church went by the name of Capt. Edward Johnson and pretended to be

in love with his landlord's sister, to whom he was to be marry'd in a day or two: but taking her out in a coach to the Red House on the strand for the air, after they had got something to eat, he died suddenly. He made his mistress a present of several rich diamonds, which prove to be only Kerry stones; and gave his landlord several sham-bills to lay by for him, making him his agent to receive eight hundred pounds *per annum* of his estate, as he said, in the county of Cork. His corpse was put into a deal-coffin, and carry'd by four porters to St Mary's church-yard; where he was buried in a Christian manner, which is more than he deserv'd. He has been marry'd to about 40 women in England and Ireland; play'd a great many cheating tricks in London; was whipped in Bridewell, spun hemp there, made his escape thence along a common-sewer &c. He was well known all over England, tho' by other names than his own.[18]

Little is known of Hurly's family background although the *Appendix* and *Innocence Justify'd* made references to Cork origins and how the family were transplanted to Clare following the Cromwellian settlement. In both the Inchiquin Papers and the state papers Hurly was described as a financial functionary in the Jacobite regime, and it was said that he had been in France from the end of 1691 until 1697 or thereabouts. It also seems that he was involved in financial and gambling escapades in France and Holland.

Donat O'Brien was a scion of one of the oldest and most respected families in Co. Clare; the O'Briens claimed descent from the Irish king Brian Boru.[19] O'Brien was the son of Conor O'Brien of Leamaneh and Máire Rua MacMahon and he was only 9 when his father was killed in a skirmish with Cromwellian troops. Shortly afterwards, in a stratagem clearly aimed at preserving the family estates, his mother married, as her third husband, John Cooper, a Cromwellian soldier. In 1663 O'Brien was declared an innocent papist, thereby copper-fastening his family's ownership of their estates. In *Innocence Justify'd* Hurly, always willing to spread any scandal that suited his cause, cast this turn of events in the worst possible light when he claimed that a child born around the time of her third marriage was fathered by the Cromwellian soldier Sir Henry Ingoldsby (1622–71), thereby making the marriage to Cooper a double marriage of convenience.

> Some Days ago, Patrick Hurley, the notorious Cheat, (who came into this Kingdom about four Months since, and to this City about five Weeks ago) took Lodgings near St. Mary's Church, went by the Name of Capt. Edward Johnson, and pretended to be in Love with his Landlord's Sister, to whom he was to be marry'd, in a Day or two: But taking her out in a Coach to the Red-House on the Strand for the Air, after they had got something to eat, he died suddenly. He made his Mistress a Present of several rich Diamonds, which prove to be only Kerry Stones; and gave his Landlord several Sham-Bills to lay by for him, making him his Agent to receive eight hundred Pounds per Annum of his Estate, as he said, in the County of Cork. His Corpse was put into a Deal-Coffin, and carry'd by four Porters to St. Mary's Church-yard; where he was buried in a Christian Manner, which is more than he deserv'd. He has been marry'd to about 40 Women in England and Ireland; play'd a great many Cheating Tricks in London; was whipt in Bridewell, spun Hemp there, made his Escape thence along a Common-Sewer, &c. He was well known all over England, tho' by other Names than his own.

6. Report on the death of Patrick Hurly (*Evening Post* (Dublin), 28 Jan. 1716)

O'Brien was the first member of his branch of the family to conform to the established church. He was created a baronet in 1686 by King James. During the Jacobite/Williamite wars, O'Brien, like many Tory-inclined Catholic or crypto-Catholic families, sought, not entirely successfully, to steer a middle course. What is certain is that he had been appointed sherriff of County Clare, by King James, although he always asserted that this had been done without his permission. In April 1690, acting apparently under the direct orders of Tyrconnell, he raised a small cavalry detachment by confiscating horses from the local gentry. O'Brien claimed that his squadron was not part of the Jacobite forces and that it had been deployed only to defend his property and that of his neighbours from the depravations of rapparees in the perilous wartime conditions. O'Brien survived Hurly's challenge. He had been MP for Clare from 1695 and until 1713 he continued to serve in parliament, where he was regarded as a Tory.

He was made a privy councillor in 1711. O'Brien was married twice. His first wife Lucia (d. 1676) was the daughter of Sir George Hamilton from a Scottish Catholic family. In 1677 he married Elizabeth Deane, daughter of a Cromwellian soldier. His son Lucius (1674–1717), who pre-deceased his father by some ten months in 1717, was MP for Clare. Lucius had married the daughter of the leading government official Thomas Keightly, who was related to the earls of Clarendon thereby cementing the close ties of this branch of the O'Brien family with the highest echelons of Irish and English society. O'Brien was reputed to be an astute financial manager, and by 1700 he was considered one of the richest commoners in Ireland. Throughout this period he added several major purchases from the Commissioners for the Sale of Forfeited Estates. In the mid-1680s O'Brien relocated the principal family seat from Leamaneh to Dromoland in Newmarket on Fergus. O'Brien was the ancestor of the subsequent baronets, many of whom were MPs for Clare. Dromoland was the home of O'Brien descendants until the 1960s when it was sold to US businessman Bernard McDonough and turned into a five-star hotel. O'Brien is buried in Kilnassoolagh Church of Ireland church. His rather over-the-top and tasteless monument, which shows a reclining figure in full formal dress of the period, was erected by his second son Henry. The lengthy inscription is fulsome in its praise for his honesty, dignity and prudence and as to how he 'Lived not for himself and his alone, but for others, but for his country'.[20] He never lost his connections to the old Gaelic aristocratic tradition, and he was the subject of two praise poems by the renowned Clare poet Aodh 'Buí' MacCrúitín (c.1680–1755).[21]

THE VERDICT AND THE SENTENCING

Following a lengthy summing up by the judge (seven pages out of fifty-six), the jury retired and after half an hour they returned to declare Hurly guilty on both counts. Before judgment was passed, Mr Butler, one of the prosecution lawyers, commented 'I hope my lord, if it be only a fine; it can't be less than the sum he designed to get from the country by the perjury'. Butler was to be disappointed; the judge ruled that 'Mr Hurly be fined for the perjury 100*l*. and be

THE
TRYAL
AND
CONVICTION
OF
Patrick Hurly:
Late of *Moughna*, in the County of
CLARE, Gent.

In his Majefty's Court of *King's-Bench* in *Ireland*, the 31ft of *May* 1701, upon *Two* (*feveral*) *Inditments*; the one for *Perjury*, and the other for Confpiring with *Daniel Hicky*, *Daniel Carty*, *Donogh ó Bryen*, *Andrews junior*, and other Malefactors Falfly and Fraudulently to Cheat the Popifh Inhabitants of the County of *Clare*, of the Summ of 1202 *l.* 9 *fhill.* fterl. By Colour of an Act of Parliament lately made in *Ireland* Intituled, *An Act for the better* Suppreffing *Tories, Robbers, Rappareees*, &c.

To which are Added

An Appendix: Being an Anfwer to a *Libel* Intituled Patrick Hurly's Vindication, with fome Remarkable PASSAGES of his *LIFE* and *ACTIONS*.

DUBLIN: Printed by *J. Whalley*, and are to be Sold at his Houfe next Door to the *Fleece* in St. *Nicholas-ftreet*, and by *Mat. Gunne* Book-feller at the *Bible* and *Crown* in *Effex-ftreet*. 1701.

7. Title page of the Dublin edition of *The tryal and conviction of Patrick Hurly: late of Moughna in the county of Clare, gent* (Dublin, 1701)

AN APPENDIX:

BEING AN

ANSWER

TO A

LIBEL,

INTITULED

Patrick Hurly's

VINDICATION:

with Some Remarkable PASSAGES of his
LIFE and *ACTIONS*.

———*Monstrum nullâ virtute redemptum
a vitiis.* Juven. 4. ———

DUBLIN, Printed by *J. Walley*, and are to be Sold at his House in St. *Nicholas-Street* ; and by *Mat. Gunne*, Bookseller, in *Essex-Street*, 1701.

8. Title page of *An appendix, being an answer to a Libel intituled Patrick Hurly's Vindication: with some remarkable passages of his life and actions* (Dublin, 1701)

Innocence Justify'd;

OR, THE
CORRECTION
OF AN
Infamous LIBEL,
CALLED THE
Tryal & Conviction
OF
Patrick Hurly, &c.

Publiſhed without Licenſe by *Gunn, Whalley*, &c. together, with a direct Paragraphical ANSWER, to a moſt Scandalous Pamphlet, Entituled, *The Appendix*, &c. ſuppos'd to be Writ by Order of Sir *Donogh O Bryen*.

Extra noxam ſum, ſed non eſt facile purgatu,
——*abunde fabularum audivimus.*

Printed in the Year MDCCI.

9. Title page of *Innocence justify'd, or; The correction of an infamous libel called the Tryal & conviction of Patrick Hurly &c.* (Dublin, 1701)

imprisoned until he pay it to the king'. The attorney general then informed the court that he would 'move the court next *Monday* for your judgment upon the other indictment ... and ... my lord, we shall insist upon it, that the pillory is the punishment for the cheat'. The court simply replied 'we know if Mr Hurly be not able to pay the fine, how he ought to suffer corporal punishment'. As mentioned elsewhere, it is not clear whether Hurly paid the fine or suffered the corporal punishment.

Was Hurly guilty, beyond a reasonable doubt, as charged? It was certainly not an open-and-shut case. The evidence as recounted in the *Tryal* is complex, opaque and hotly disputed on almost every point (fig. 7). The state, for its own broader security and political considerations, was certainly keen to secure a conviction and various agents put in much time and effort to secure the conviction. There is no doubt that Hurly was a career cheat and a liar. It is also clear that in the early months of 1700 he was in severe financial difficulty and needed some way out. While evidence for the early ideation of a scheme to claim compensation from the county and for the existence of fake counters was presented, it can be considered problematic and, like much of the prosecution's evidence, it was strongly disputed. The testimony of the alleged robbers is even more problematic. It is almost certain that, despite denials by the JPs and the gaoler in Ennis, the robbers/accomplices were subjected to at least implicit threats and perhaps to financial blandishments. Yet in the final analysis they stuck to their story. The possibility of simmering local disputes between Hurly and O'Brien and with Capt. Lynch as motivating factors, while alluded to, were not central to the prosecution's case, which retained a strong focus on the financial motivation and in proving the sham robbery and fraud hypothesis. The parallel process in which Hurly sought to have O'Brien tried for treason was not alluded to in the trial testimony, although it was dealt with in detail in both the *Appendix* (fig. 8) and Hurly's *Innocence Justify'd* (fig. 9). For the jury, as Protestants, they would not have to pay the compensation, so in theory they did not have any economic motivation not to accept Hurly's story and thereby to allow the compensation claim, which would have had the effect of burdening the Catholic taxpayers with the cost. But equally there is little doubt that, as alleged by Hurly, some of them would have had some form of dependence, either directly or indirectly, on the economic heft of the local magnate O'Brien. For Hurly, if the compensation claim was to fail, turning 'informer' was a career option that might yield rich rewards; a letter from Samuel Twiford informed O'Brien on 9 August 1700 that 'Mr Hy speaks bigg ... he says the trustees have agreed to pay him £15,000 for his share of your estate'.

3. The case of Patrick Hurly in law, in politics and in print

The case of Patrick Hurly was something of a contemporary Irish *cause célèbre* across the three separate but connected spheres of law, politics and print. It necessitated the deployment of the full resources of the state including several illustrious MPs and numerous other officials locally in Clare, in Dublin and even in London. They gathered evidence in respect of the sham robbery and followed up Hurly's treason allegations against Donat O'Brien (fig. 10). In December 1700 the Privy Council and the lords justices seriously considered the possibility of placing O'Brien on trial for treason and the Hurly affair became one of the first fully Irish-based criminal-trial pamphlet wars.

HURLY IN LAW

The trial lasted just one, albeit long, day and involved both a significant quantum of complex and conflicting evidence. Was it a fair trial; was justice served? What does the Hurly trial tell us about the working of the legal system in early eighteenth-century Ireland? At a procedural level, the printed text of the *Tryal* provides an unusually clear window onto the quotidian process of criminal trials in Ireland. While trial procedures at the time bore some resemblance to current practice, there were also major and important differences. One main difference was that while the jury, as in modern trials, was charged with deciding on the facts, and in civil cases on the level of the award that might be granted to the aggrieved party, most of the questioning of witnesses during the fact-finding process within the trial was led by the judge and not by counsel for the prosecution or defence. In the *Tryal* text, when the prosecution or defence wanted to make sure that a point of evidence that they believed to be crucial to their side of the

10. Sir Donat O'Brien, 1st baronet of Leamaneh (1642–1717) (source: Mary Beale, Dromoland Castle)

argument was fully explored they would ask the judge to question the witness. A good example was when Sir John Meade requested the court to ask Cornelius Carty whether he had ever been 'tampered with to take off your evidence', which Justice Coote proceeded to do. In this period most trials, both civil and criminal, were taken at the initiative of the aggrieved party and state prosecutions were a relative rarity, being for the most part concerned with such state matters as treason and counterfeiting. In the early decades of the eighteenth century the presence of professional counsel, either for the prosecution or for the defence, was a rarity. Indeed, there was a longstanding judicial prohibition against their appearance, other than to advise on issues of law. For centuries, English criminal procedure adhered to the 'principle that a person accused of a serious crime should not be represented by counsel at trial'.[1] The adversarial lawyer-led scenario with which we are familiar, with its complex rules of admissible evidence (especially hearsay), became the norm only from the last decades of the eighteenth century. This is not to say that judges and lawyers were unaware of the dangers inherent in the potential for juries to be suborned and/or influenced by local elites (the risk of witnesses for hire), and for obviously tainted evidence to be presented without question. The Irish-born English judge James Comyn noted that 'a feature of the Hurly case was that there was a splendid disregard for the rules of evidence and procedure which we have come to venerate'.[2] The Hurly trial is therefore somewhat unusual in the extent to which both sides were well represented: six counsel for the prosecution (including four MPs) and three for the defence (including two MPs). Likewise, the question of who paid for it all is unclear. Given the state of Hurly's finances, it hardly seems likely that he could have paid his legal expenses, to say nothing of the costs associated with the production of two pamphlets. The subject of such a payment was mentioned only once during the trial when Hurly queried one witness (Donogh O'Brien Andrews senior, the father of one of the alleged robbers): 'Pray whose horse, and whose expense brought him here? ... at whose charge?', to which the witness replied 'at the county's charge, who prosecuted you for perjury'. It is also important to note that in this period defendants were not permitted to testify. The logic of this stricture was that the defendant would inevitably give false evidence (perjure themselves) in their anxiety to avoid conviction. This rule was strictly adhered to, and it was relaxed only at the end of the nineteenth century. In this instance it is somewhat ironic given that the essence of a perjury trial is the accusation of having given false evidence. During the trial in one of only a handful of personal interjections when Hurly sought to reject the evidence of Walter Neylan on the basis that he would be unlikely to ask Neylan for help: 'my lord, this is a man that is in trouble for me, and bound to Thomas Arthur on my account'. At this point the court, upholding the rule of no testimony from the accused, interjected 'Mr Hurly, you are a man of parts, and you know what is us'd to be done in this kind; if you please, you may have pen, ink and paper to take notes and, when it comes to your turn, you shall ask what questions you please'.

As per normal practice it fell to Judge Coote to sum up and to direct the jury. His summation, which ran to over seven pages, was an impressive performance especially if it was prepared from the notes he had taken over the course of the day. As he had played an important role in parts of the pre-trial investigation process, Coote would have been familiar with much of the detail. Nevertheless, it must be acknowledged that his summation was, for the most part, an accurate, complete and fair summary of the trial evidence. There was a bias towards the prosecution, however, in that the judge asked the jury to take into consideration the 'credit' of the various witnesses. He opened his remarks with what could be termed a standard judicial admonition: 'gentlemen of the jury you have heard a very long evidence, and I will repeat the heads of it to you as well as I can, that you may discharge yourselves with honour and conscience: you have taken an oath, and I hope you will not be led to perverting of justice one way or other'. He concluded with a similarly standard admonition:

> I do but lay the Facts before you as they stand upon the evidence, as for as against the prisoner; and I hope you will do justice both to the prisoner and to the king, gentlemen, if you are satisfied upon the whole matter, that Mr Hurly is guilty of the perjury, you will find him guilty; if not, you will acquit him. If you think him guilty of contrivance to cheat the country, you will bind him guilty; if not, you will acquit him.

A further question arises at this point; can we trust the content of the *Tryal* text? It is nowhere stated that the printed text is a complete verbatim report, although the format implies as much. While the golden age of shorthand lay sometime in the future, various systems of shorthand were available and were used to make notes of both court and parliamentary proceedings in this period; so it would have been possible to generate such a text in real time.[3] The respected legal historian and Swift scholar Francis Elrington Ball, in his monumental *Judges of Ireland* from 1927, believed that the Hurly trial text was a credible source. He described it as 'the most illuminating survival of that period'. He also noted that 'as trials then lasted never more than a day, it is probably a fairly full one, and is certainly sufficiently full to afford some idea of the procedure'.[4] Comyn estimated that it must have lasted up to twelve hours. At the end the attorney general commented ''tis now growing late, and I will not take up more time in summing up this long evidence to the jury, but leave it to the court'. Within the text there are no examples of what might be termed stage guidelines and so it is hard to get a sense of the theatrical and performative aspects of what must have been a rather dramatic occasion. As expected, the language of the legal professionals, on both sides, fitted the expected formality of a court session and the text is replete with legal phrases such as 'may it please your lordship', 'my lord and you gentlemen of the jury' and the prosecution's invocation to witnesses to 'tell the whole truth and nothing but the truth'. All witnesses were sworn in and the court drew attention to this fact on several occasions over the course of the day.[5] The questioning of witnesses was, for the most part, brief and firmly focused on the relevant evidentiary point. For example, Alderman Samuel Walton's testimony would have lasted a couple of moments as he apparently answered only four questions in respect of Hurly's financial affairs and of rumours of valuable jewellery that Hurly had allegedly brought back from France in 1697. There was almost no repeated or forensic questioning of witnesses on the minutiae of the point being presented, even when the testimony seems to be ambiguous or opaque, and on occasion to the point of incomprehensibility. Almost all the questioning of witnesses was done by the judge; referred to as the court throughout the text, although there were occasional direct interventions by members of both the prosecution and the defence teams. It is also clear from the

Tryal text that at least some of the witnesses had heard the evidence of previous witnesses and on several occasions witnesses, who were still under oath, were asked supplemental questions in response to later testimony, to which they apparently responded from the body of the court. Frustratingly, within the testimony the chronology of events, and the exact dates for many events that are alleged to have occurred were rarely stated with precision. For example, John Crips testified that he was approached/tampered with 'about three weeks after Mr Hurly was taken to Ennis' and that a later incident was 'about six weeks after Hurly was taken'. At no point was the exact date for these events attested.

Despite the legal formality of the trial process, some members of the legal teams were not above wry humour. When examining Mortagh Mac Colloghy about the attempted passing of some of the gold counters by Hickey's wife for the purchase of a strayed cow, Hurly's counsel had somewhat tendentiously queried how the cow had gone astray. The solicitor general reposted 'we cannot tell you, you may examine the cow, the cow know best'. Only one witness, Capt. Lynch, expressed some irritation at being summoned to the hearing when in response to a question as to whether he was a relation of Hurly's he replied 'I have friendship for him, and if I had known I was to be summon'd, I would not have been within forty miles of this place this day'. As ever in criminal trials, there were direct and, in the end, irreconcilable conflicts in the evidence and on one occasion when such a divergence was acute the judge simply noted 'when a man tells you on his oath that he cannot tell; and we can't make a man swear more than he can swear'.[6]

What about the charge? Perjury had been recognized as a common-law offence since an Elizabethan statute of 1563.[7] While perjury was still categorized as a misdemeanour, it was nonetheless one of ten categories of crime that were categorized as 'of publick offences committed against the king and the people', which became state trials. Eighteenth-century jurists writing on perjury were primarily concerned with the dangers posed by lying witnesses. Despite the pillory being the usual punishment for perjury, a fate that befell Redmond Joy in 1703 (see below), James Oldham has claimed that 'the "threat" of the perjury prosecution was largely impotent as a counterforce to the abuses of witnesses for hire'.[8] Securing a conviction for perjury due to the falsity of sworn testimony in an affidavit was not unknown however. For example, *The Proceedings of the Old Bailey* record 1,781 instances of trials for perjury, of which 286 were for perjury on foot of sworn testimony.[9] And in 1698 William Argent, alias John Warner, was indicted for perjury upon an affidavit sworn before a justice of the peace. He was ordered to stand three times in the pillory and fined 6*l*. 13*s*.

HURLY IN POLITICS

In the 1690s and the early decades of the eighteenth century the fear of Jacobite conspiracy was a real phenomenon; it was not just the stuff of ultra-Protestant paranoid nightmares. As Ó Ciardha demonstrated in his *Ireland and the Jacobite cause, 1685–1766: a fatal attachment*, there is little doubt that Jacobitism was the dominant ideology of the residual Catholic elite and most likely within elements of the crypto-Catholic elite, even if most were not prepared to be open in providing active support.[10] The very real invasion scares of 1692 and 1696, and the memory of the admittedly feeble but nonetheless traumatizing abortive assassination plot of 1696 against the king served to keep the Jacobite threat in the forefront of the minds of those inclined to fret over such matters.[11] With the wisdom of hindsight, and taking account the impact of the defeat at La Hogue, we now know that the military and conspiratorial capabilities, and at times the organizational competency, of both continental and local Jacobitism may have been overestimated. But the Irish law officers of the 1690s and the first decades of the eighteenth century could not have known this. Therefore, despite the intimacy of O'Brien's political and familial connections, it is not surprising that in the autumn and winter of 1700–1 Hurly's allegations against him were afforded more than a passing level of consideration in Dublin Castle and that in the fullness of time they were relayed onto London. The appointment in 1699, by the authorities in London, of the Commissioners appointed to Enquire into the Forfeited Estates of Ireland generated a renewed interest in such matters. Rooting out Jacobites and identifying those not yet found guilty of treason from the 'late troubles', or those who should not be availing of what many perceived as the generous terms of the various surrender articles was a priority. In 1698 Sir Francis Brewster (MP and member of the commission) expressed a fear that 'under the subterfuge of the articles of Limerick, Galway etc. [Catholics] have sheltered themselves from common justice, and live splendidly and securely on spoils of ruined Protestants'.[12] The discovery of yet another assassination plot involving Redmond Joy from 1703 (and in which Hurly was involved) was but another example of the numerous leads that were assiduously followed up by the ever-vigilant authorities. Ó Ciardha set the accusations against O'Brien in the context of the phenomenon of Protestant Jacobitism and in particular how 'the abortive invasion of 1692 provides a context for the witch-hunt against the Protestant landowner and Clare magnate Sir Donat O'Brien'.

The problem was that the investigation of these conspiracies almost always involved the unsavoury and unsatisfactory presence of paid informers/discoverers. In this period, and in the absence of an investigative policing capability, making payments for information was a central plank of the legal system in most European countries. This practice has been much criticized, both then and since; in 1957 it was colourfully described by M.W. Beresford as a 'marriage of justice with malice or avarice'.[13] Even in an age that displayed somewhat less concern for the rights of the accused than today, this practice still presented the authorities with a dilemma. It is not that there was unwillingness on their part to be tough and so, for example, they were more than willing to carry out illegal, or at best semi-legal, actions, such as intercepting post and both the state papers and the Inchiquin Papers contain numerous references to how Hurly's letters had been intercepted in the post office. In January 1701 Hurly's letter to his brother in London was 'taken up at the post office there' and in the same month Hurly persuaded Richard Roche, a fellow prisoner in the Marshalsea, to send letters and packages to his sister in London so 'it might come safe to the person to whom it was intended'. The reality was that the use of such dubious sources of information as the cornerstone of the prosecution case presented an obvious credibility challenge. The senior law officers and judges such as Rochfort, Brodrick and Coote had a duty, and often a personal interest, in tracking down valid cases of Jacobite conspiracies and their political opponents would certainly ensure that any accusations of being soft on Jacobites would have exposed them to criticism in parliament and at court. The problem was that the source of such information was at best tainted with personal interest, often laced with deep local and familial animosities, and on occasion by full-on criminal intent. The evidence that had been secured from such sources was most likely to be problematic and there was real risk that such evidence was unlikely to stand up in court if even a modicum of due process and cross examination was allowed, all the more so if, as in the case of O'Brien, the accused was of high status and well-connected and if they had secured the services of leading/competent lawyers.

In this context, Hurly was by no means unique in his attempts to persuade authorities that he was in possession of strategically important intelligence against covert Jacobites. In May 1699 the lord justice, Henri de Massue, earl of Galway (1648–1720), writing to James Vernon (1646–1727), secretary of state in London, made several references to a Mr Lloid (perhaps Lloyd?) who he was using as an investigator of accusations of Jacobitism against leading political and landed figures. Galway had decidedly mixed views about Lloid: 'I could not avoid giving Lloid a recommendation to you; forgive me for doing so; he is the best of those people that I have come across'. The correspondence concerned accusations levelled by Redmond Joy against the Limerick magnate Thady Quin of Adare (1646–1727) where Galway noted 'I think Lloid is not far wrong about Thady Quine; but there was so much perjury, and so much else that was reprehensible when these cases were pleaded before the Court of Claims, that I admit I have great difficulty in coming to any conclusion'. He continued

> Redman Joy is very ill spoken of; one cannot believe what they say. These are inevitable and most unprofitable importunities. They complain of being discouraged because they are not paid what they ask, which must not be given to them. One must not be exposed to the reproach of having suborned witnesses.

The spectacular failure of the so-called Lancashire Plot case in 1694 would have provided a recent and embarrassing example of how a conspiracy-theory mentality, combined with a surfeit of imagination and the use of problematical evidence sourced from disreputable characters could end.[14] Rachel Weil's *A plague of informers: conspiracy and political trust in William III's England* from 2013 stresses the issue of what constituted credibility in this period and the perennial fear that the need for and the use of such testimony would irredeemably corrupt the legal process.[15] Nevertheless, as Ó Ciardha has concluded, 'the discovery of personal conflicts does not always deprive such testimony of its value in reflecting an atmosphere of sedition from which it derives its credibility'. Hurly had succeeded in getting the attention of the authorities with his accusations against O'Brien but he failed to produce the required evidence to a standard that would pass muster in a court of law.

The conviction of Hurly and his confederates in May 1701 was not the end of Hurly in politics however. In 1703 Joy and Hurly were jointly mentioned when on 5 June Southwell, writing to Nottingham, in London, noted

> I was ordered by his grace to go this afternoon with the lord chief justice and attorney general to the prison to hear the discovery of one Redmond Joy relating to a design against her Majesty's person by one Patrick Hurly and others now in London. The lord chief justice is drawing up the examination, and intends to send to-night for some persons mentioned by Joy ... I should not lose a minute in a matter of so high a nature were it not that the informant is a man who, only four days ago, was 'pilloried for a notorious perjury and forgery, and one of his ears cut close off', and that he has been concerned in plots and plot-making for years and has tired the government here with the trouble as well as the charge of his informations. However, since what he proposes is the taking up of some loose fellows, who are some of his former gang, it will be easily seen what credit may be given thereto.

Some days later on 8 June Southwell noted

> I now enclose the papers relating to Redmond Joy mentioned in my last. The first is his letter to my Lord Dike, the paper is what my L.C. Justice Pyne collected from the examination, & that of Hurly's Wife, the 3rd is another paper from Joy to my L.C.

Justice of what witnesses he has in Kerry to prove this matter. It will with submission be very proper to have Patrick Hurly taken up, for he is certainly a very great rogue, & has broke Gaol her in the Queens debt upon a fine, so that were he here or sent over, wee have enough against him. ... for being in confederacy to swear several people out of their estates. ... Upon the whole matter I must repeat to your Lord^{sh} the opinion of every one here, that if he had mentioned anything but a matter of the highs moment, noe notice would be taken of him.

HURLY IN PRINT

The publication of the Hurly *Tryal* text was a first in Irish legal publishing history. Few detailed accounts of Irish criminal trials, let alone a printed edition that appeared to be a full trial transcript of such a high-profile case, survive from the early years of the eighteenth century. In *Innocence Justify'd* Hurly alleged that it had been 'published without license' and that

> the court of king's bench was pleas'd on the 14th instant November publickly to resent the injury done its honour and sense in the publication of the unlicenced tryal and that for that misdemeanour, the two chief support and publishers of *Sir Donough's* fame and loyalty; *Whalley* the printer and *Gunn* the bookseller were bound-over, to be prosecuted in that court.

As previously noted, contemporaneously with the publication of the *Tryal*, and no doubt with the financial support of O'Brien, the *Appendix* was also published in Dublin. The stated aim of the *Appendix* was to put on the record a rebuttal to the claims that Hurly had made in his (so far) untraced pamphlet. From O'Brien's perspective, the danger was that Hurly's text published 'in the critical time, to forerun and usher in the tryal' would succeed in setting the agenda, and in arousing 'compassion and pity' among a gullible public. Following Hurly's conviction, however, the author of the *Appendix* confidently declared that the clear light shone on these events by the verdict of the trial had caused Hurly's 'libel' to expire 'that very night' and he continued 'nor is the place of its burial know to the very day'. In the autumn of 1701 it may have been the case that O'Brien, and possibly other members of the convert and crypto-Catholic landed elite, feared that Hurly's published version of events might live on in the public sphere and in the public imagination and that a printed rebuttal was required. Whatever the intention, the publication of the *Tryal* and the *Appendix* in turn resulted in Hurly publishing a further fifty-page riposte. The irony is that no copies of Hurly's first pamphlet seem to have survived and only one copy (missing eight pages) of his riposte. As a literary text, the *Appendix* is not a success; the tone is moralizing throughout and by times the text is turgid, opaque and almost incomprehensible. Throughout, the author displays a disdainful and condescending sense of hauteur and snobbery in respect of Hurly's antecedents. He took Hurly to task for declaring himself an esquire, a claim he says was based on Hurly having at some point attended the Inns of Court in London; although being a Catholic he was never called to the bar. The author dismissed this by averring that if this 'were admitted to be sufficient the number of esquires would crowd, grow over-cheap, and fall into contempt among us'. Such unauthorized claims were presented as just another example of Hurly's 'counterfeits', 'fraud' and 'robbery'. Nevertheless, the title of the printed *Tryal* referred to Hurly as Gent and, as already noted, the state records of Irish Jacobites had listed Hurly as an esquire. The condescension of Hurly and his antecedents is repeated where the Hurly family, previously known as 'Murihilly', and originally from Carbery in Co. Cork, are described as but 'a peasantly obscure family', part of the 'dependents or followers of Mac Carty Reagh'. It was alleged that the Hurlys moved to Clare as part of the Cromwellian transplantations but, as they appear not to have been granted an estate in Clare, the author of the *Appendix* infers, perhaps somewhat tendentiously, that they therefore had no estate in Cork. He also raised the issue of their less-than-clear entitlement to the lease of the farm at Moughna, which apparently was only held in trust by Hurly's father for the use of his daughter who was married to Daniel Hickey.

Essentially, the *Appendix* is a forty-page character assassination. The core argument was that if the veracity of some specific points could be challenged then why should anyone 'suspect him of truth anywhere'. The *Appendix* highlighted Hurly's numerous financial and amorous affairs, his frequent cheats in business, his serial need to escape from his creditors in France, Holland, London and Ireland, and his frauds as an army agent in France and as a forager in the service of King James in Dublin and Limerick. Hurly's serial resort to the use of multiple aliases also came in for criticism, and especially his projection of himself as the Count of Mountcallan. The accusation was that Hurly was always a lying cheat and a rogue, and that this was a pattern that started in 'his tender years'. The author delighted in relating a story of how Hurly, as a youth, had reputedly stolen some coins from his mother by taking them in his mouth and then hiding them. When he was accosted by his mother the youngster declared somewhat Jesuitically on oath that 'he never handled the money'. The *Appendix* also attempted to deploy a rather clumsy humour, such as the story of how Hurly's 'debauching' of a local girl with an insincere promise to marry her, following which he was sent to France to study in the Irish college in Bordeaux where 'He was indeed desig'd for the priesthood, and consequently for celibacy, for which it may confess'd he was wonderfully qulify'd'. While in France Hurly was accused of selling fake certificates from the college and that 'by this means the Irish became so over-stock'd with ordinary clergy'. Traducing Hurly's character, however, could get the author only so far. At their core, Hurly's accusations against O'Brien were twofold. First, that O'Brien was guilty of treason and that he could prove the involvement of Sir Donat as one of the Irish conspirators in the run up to the abortive La Hogue invasion of 1692.[16] The author of the *Appendix* dismissed this later accusation in a single sentence by pointing out the improbability of Hurly having had access to such strategic secrets as the 'conspirators were so wary in France ... that their counsels and resolves were kept as private and close, as is usual in such cases in any court in Europe' with the ironic conclusion 'the French only excepted'. Hurly's further accusation was that O'Brien had organized the robbery to impoverish Hurly and thereby force him to flee the country to avoid his creditors, but when O'Brien discovered that Hurly might succeed in reclaiming the loss from the county he was forced to devise a new strategy – to suborn the robbers and have Hurly convicted of perjury. Again, this is dismissed in short order as fanciful, as if the denial was sufficient. Notwithstanding the verbal bluster of the *Appendix*, the reality was that in late 1700 and early 1701, as is shown by the papers in the Inchiquin archive and the state papers, O'Brien had to provide rather more firm evidence to the forfeited estates commissioners and he had to use his social network to bolster his argument that he was not involved in the Jacobite plots of the 1690s.

Late in 1701 Hurly replied with a fifty-page rebuttal, *Innocence Justify'd*. The frontispiece has a Latin epigram *extra noxam sum, sed non es facile purgatu, abunde fabularum audivimus*, which can be translated loosely as 'while I might be out of harm's way, it is not so easy to clear away the dirt, we have heard a lot of stories'. Akin to the *Appendix*, *Innocence Justify'd* is also something of a hard read although the literary standard is higher. For example, in the preface he invoked the story of Guzman d'Alfarache Lazarillo de Tormes, the picaresque novel of an anti-hero coming of age against all the odds. This was followed by a reference to a similar well-known early novel *The English Rogue* by the Irish author Richard Head (c.1637–pre-1686).[17] Much of the text consisted of abuse and name calling. Examples included referring to O'Brien as 'the mirrour of knighthood', 'a second rate jobber' and 'my grand persecutor', and the anonymous author of the *Appendix* as 'a hackney ruffian' and 'a degraded member of that gown which the song says, Can prove pease and beans to be bacon &c.' On occasion, Hurly conceded some points, such as his use of the alias of 'count or earl of Montcallan', which he justified as a necessary bluff to gain access to elite gatherings as part of his spying missions for King James. On occasion, the accusations can be both personal and salacious, the most scurrilous being his character assassination of O'Brien's mother, where Hurly claimed

> as to the old man's stock (as the libeller stiles my father) Red Mary McMahon, Sur Donogh's mother ... for her condition was then so miserably poor, that she had no way to support her, and the many children she had by her first husband, Daniel Neylan, and by Sir Donogh's father but to go about as a distressed widow according to the Irish custom to patrol and beg cows, sheep and corn; till at length being a buxom comely woman, and happening to beg of Sir Harry Ingoldsby, then a leading man in muster, he gave her a nine month's belly-full, and then prevail'd upon one John Cooper, a broken cornet, to marry

her. For the truth hereof, I refer the reader to all the ancient inhabitants of the county of Clare, and more particularly to Mr Matthew McMahon of Tuogh and Mr Timothy McDonogh of Bally keal, who can likewise affirm that my father whom the scribbler would represent for a peasant, was a man of better sense, courage, parts, person and at least of as much honesty as Sir Donogh, and brought a plentiful fortune with him to the county.

As would be expected, Hurly made what he could of any inconsistencies in the witness testimonies and especially the threats made to the alleged robbers; he claimed that 'What facts were deficient, he had orders to supply with invention' and that the *Appendix* was nothing but a 'spin-text'; an accusation of which he could be accused of being equally guilty. Hurly asserted that O'Brien had sent his minions out to the Dublin bookshops to buy up all the stock; perhaps they succeeded too well as to date no copy has been located and strangely there is no copy of *Hurly's vindication* in the Inchiquin archive.

It can be argued that this flurry of print was the first, albeit rather minor, Irish-based criminal-trial pamphlet war. Given the relatively small number of pamphlets involved, it should perhaps be termed a 'pamphlet skirmish'. The *Tryal* was the first instance of the printing of a complete transcript of an Irish criminal trial by a Dublin printer. Two decades earlier, at the height of the Popish plot in England, there had been a flurry of Dublin re-printings of London editions of some of the sensational trial texts, including that of Archbishop Oliver Plunkett.[18] The Hurly trial also had an extended afterlife in print starting in 1719 when the full text of *Tryal* was reprinted in London, in what may been seen as an almost textbook example of a trial text for use by practising lawyers. Perhaps reflecting the level of evidential detail and given that it was state prosecution, the *Tryal* text (or abridged versions thereof) appeared in numerous editions of the multi-volume *Complete collection of state-trials and proceedings upon high-treason and other crimes and misdemeanours* published in London from 1719 until the nineteenth century.[19] Three editions of these volumes were published in Dublin in 1737, 1741 and 1793. In both the 1730 edition of state-trials and an edition from nearly a century later in

1816, the Hurly case was the only Irish one reported on for the reigns of William III and Anne.[20] It was also the only case involving a charge of perjury.

The publications associated with the Hurly affair marked an important step in the evolution of the nascent Irish printing industry, both in terms of the number of publications involved, and in the controversial subject matter, although the print quality and the literary standard of the *Appendix* and *Innocence Justify'd* leave much to be desired.[21] Both are replete with pompous and snobbish put-downs, name-calling, and opaque references to events and individuals which are hard, or on occasion impossible, to decipher. In places, they are so poorly drafted and argued that it can be difficult to take them seriously (although this is not meant to suggest that they are somehow parodies or satirical works). The Dublin edition of the *Tryal* was published by John Whalley (1653–1724) and the title page announced that they 'are to be sold at his house, and by Mat Gunne'. Whalley and Gunne (1684–1724) were well-known colourful figures in the expanding world of Dublin printing and bookselling. Whalley was originally from London, but from 1682 he was resident in Dublin, where he was active as a stationer, astrologer and publisher of almanacs and later editor and printer of a series of newspapers under various titles (all of which displayed a strong Whig bias). He, like several other printers in early eighteenth-century Dublin, was also involved in the sale of quack medicines, elixirs and pills.[22] He described himself as Dr Whalley but this was not an acknowledgment of any medical training or even competence. Robert Munter, the historian of early Irish newspapers, described how these early publishers were 'resourceful, innovative stationers, who in their search for any possible money-making schemes came to experiment with newspapers, proved to be the pioneers of the Irish periodical press'.[23] It is not clear why O'Brien, a first-generation Protestant from an ancient Gaelic family and with a questionable Tory/Jacobite past and who was under active investigation for treasonous Jacobitism by the Dublin authorities, would have chosen such a controversial Whig printer. Given Hurly's claim that the printers had been harassed for the publication, it is unlikely that they had done so on their own initiative. From the late 1670s Gunne was a leading figure in the world of bookselling and printing in Dublin. He was also a staunch Whig and in 1698 the

London bookseller John Dunton described his as 'a firm adherer to the established government, and an enemy to *popery and slavery*'.[24] Over the course of his career, Gunne published numerous political tracts and he specialized in Dublin reprints of London anti-Catholic tracts. The Whalley–Gunne cooperation seems to have been limited to 1701 as the English Short Title Catalogue records no such cooperation in previous or later years.

In addition to the publications associated with the trial, Hurly made several other appearances in the world of eighteenth-century print. A decade after the perjury trial he was at the centre of a series of publications relating to another legal dispute, on this occasion concerning fraud in a regiment commanded by the notorious gambler and rake, Col. Francis Charteris.[25] In 1714 a highly tendentious and inaccurate twenty-six-page biography of Hurly (spelt Hurley) featured prominently in a book entitled *The memoirs of the lives, intrigues and comical adventures of the most famous gamesters and celebrated sharpers in the reigns of Charles II, James II, William III and Queen Anne* by the otherwise unknown author Theophilus Lucas. This lengthy volume was published in two editions in London in 1714 and a third edition (with no updating of the Hurly chapter) in 1744.[26] In the years after the perjury trial Hurly made several appearances in the London newspapers. In 1709 he was reported as having been indicted for 'polygamy' and as using various aliases including going by the names of William Hart and William Hickman. A reward of £10 was announced for information leading to his capture or proof of his death.[27] In May 1713 Hurly, described as 'a tall bulky fair man', was accused of stealing jewellery from Mr Daniel Shovell of Broad Street in London. A reward of £40 was offered and, curiously, 'if the said Patrick Hurly will return the said jewels, he shall have the same reward, and no questions ask'd'.[28] In October 1713 the *Post-Boy* in London reported that 'this week one Hurley was committed to Newgate for several notorious cheats'.[29]

Hurly's final appearance in contemporary sources occurred in March 1725 when 'Rickard Burke and his wife Elizabeth, administratrix of Patrick Hurley, gent. her former husband, deceased' were involved in a lengthy and complex court case with Christopher O'Brien.[30] This was in respect of a lease for lives dated 1687 from Viscount Ikerrin for land in Clare that had made its way on final appeal to the British House of Lords. The text of the printed case for the appellants, Burke and his wife, described how Hurly had intended to use the lease as a provision for his wife but that he 'was prevented by great troubles and misfortunes, which soon after he fell into, being thrown into prison, where he remained a long time, until at last he made his escape, and quitted that kingdom'. It described how in May 1700 'being then in prison, and having great occasion for 30*l*.', he used the lease as security. Following his death, which was listed as 1717, when his widow tried to assert her rights O'Brien claimed that he was a valid purchaser without notice. Burke and his wife lost their case.

Conclusion

It could be argued that the 1701 trial and conviction of Patrick Hurly for perjury and fraud were nothing more than a minor criminal affair in rural Co. Clare, albeit involving a rather large sum and firearms. The motivation could be ascribed either to the greed and avarice of the perpetrator or to local rivalries; just another incident in the disturbed conditions of post-war Ireland. But within days of the so-called 'sham robbery', as described in the prosecution of Hurly in March 1700 the Hurly affair began to become a *cause célèbre* in the Irish legal system and in contemporary politics and in due course it became an important event in the nascent Irish public sphere and the world of print. Within weeks the full resources of the state including leading MPs, senior judges and numerous other officials, both locally in Clare, then in Dublin, and by year's end in London, were employed in gathering the evidence in respect of the sham robbery and in following up on Hurly's treason allegations against O'Brien. While the Hurly imbroglio enjoys a modest presence in the historiography of the period it is deserving of a more detailed review. Within this historiography, Hurly has been represented as an unscrupulous scoundrel who 'took advantage of the condition of the people, to perform, under cover of the laws against rapparees and the penal statutes, acts which were no less barbarous and unjust'.[1] Simms has recounted how the forfeiture commissioners 'were fed by informers, of whom the most notorious was Patrick Hurley' and Ó Murchadha characterized Hurly simply as an opportunist and 'an informer'.[2] This book sets out a more detailed examination of the (inevitably incomplete) available evidence as preserved in the trial transcript, the pamphlets, the Inchiquin Papers, the state papers and contemporary newspapers, to answer a series of questions surrounding the Hurly affair. First, was Hurly guilty of perjury and attempted fraud as charged? Did the evidence stack up? Second, why was it so important to the powers that be to secure the conviction of a mid-ranking Jacobite rogue for a crime that had occurred in rural

Conclusion

Co. Clare? Third, why were both sides so intent on having their side of the story preserved in print? Fourth, where does the episode of the trial and conviction of Hurly fit into the actions and stratagems of the displaced Catholic elite and the response of the still-nervous Protestant ascendancy to this potentially existential threat? And finally, what does the evidence of the *Tryal* text and the background evidence of the Inchiquin Papers and the state papers tell us about the nature of the criminal legal system in early eighteenth-century Ireland?

One fact seems to be clear. We know from the printed *Tryal* text of 1701, published in both Dublin and London and replicated in legal textbooks for more than one hundred years thereafter, that on 31 May 1701 Patrick Hurly of Moughna, Co. Clare, Gentleman, was convicted of perjury at the court of king's bench in Dublin. He was convicted of swearing a false affidavit in respect of what was termed at his trial the 'sham robbery' of the enormous sum of £1,300. He was also convicted for conspiracy to defraud or 'cheat' the 'popish inhabitants' of Co. Clare by seeking compensation under the provisions of the Act for the Better Suppression of Tories, Robbers and Rapparees. While Hurly was undoubtedly a career cheat and a thorough scoundrel, that does not necessarily make him guilty in every circumstance. The question remains, did Hurly receive a fair trial? And can we trust the *Tryal* text as a primary source to answer this question? The legal historian Francis Elrington Ball was of the view that the trial text was 'the most illuminating survival of that period' and 'probably a fairly full one, and is certainly sufficiently full to afford some idea of the procedure'; this is certainly a positive review, if not quite a complete endorsement of either the process or of the outcome.[3] In that context, it is worth noting that, except for the use of an interpreter to translate the testimony of three monoglot Irish speakers, the Hurly *Tryal* was a totally Anglophone, common law and Protestant (and an almost exclusively male) event. In addition, it was not an overtly sectarian event. As a stand-alone record of a criminal trial, and despite Hurly's protestation of witness intimidation and of the result being pre-determined, the *Tryal* text does not bear the obvious hallmarks of a show trial or of a trial that was irredeemably compromised from the beginning either by the use of bogus evidence, a rigged jury or a biased judge; this is despite the defence assertions of malpractice on all three of these grounds and the claim of Francis Bernard, Hurly's defence counsel, that 'these prosecutions have been carried on by bribery, and such like practices'. At a procedural level, some of the comments from the bench about the sanctity of sworn testimony, and the role of the jury to weigh up the evidence as presented, would not be out of place today. We should also make allowance for what Comyn described as the 'splendid disregard for the rules of evidence and procedure which we have come to venerate' and in particular the acceptance of hearsay evidence.[4] The Hurly trial was somewhat unusual for the period in that it was a state prosecution rather than a private one. Clearly, from the perspective of the state, securing a conviction was a high priority as such an egregious breach of the intention of the rapparee acts by a Catholic Jacobite official and a well-known cheat simply could not be tolerated. Accordingly, various agents of the state put in much time and resources to secure the required result. On the day of the trial, they deployed a top-notch legal team, including the two most senior legal officers. They also arranged for a jury to be transferred from Clare and for the presence of numerous witnesses from Clare. Overall, the Hurly trial was an impressive logistical and organizational feat which no doubt cost a lot of treasure. Somehow, Hurly also manged to have access to a top legal team; how he paid for this remains unclear.

Was Hurly simply a ne'er do well who was using the rapparee acts to recover his fortune? Is it possible he had other motivations? Could disputes, even vendettas, between Hurly and O'Brien, and a potentially ruinous dispute with his immediate landlord Capt. Lynch, be background motivating factors? While these possibilities were alluded to during the trial testimony, they were not central to the prosecution case and unfortunately the evidence necessary to explore these avenues does not fully emerge in the sources. On the day of the trial the prosecution stuck resolutely to its strategy of seeking to prove Hurly's dire financial position, the existence of the fake coins and the early ideation of the plan to 'fix a robbery on the country' so that 'he could tax what sum he pleased'. It can be argued that the jury would have been capable of judging the case simply based on the evidence adduced on the day of the trial. In addition, as Protestants, they would not have been liable for the compensation, and it could even be argued that it could suit them as it would further impoverish their Catholic neighbours. But equally there is likelihood that some of the jurymen were, as alleged by Hurly, dependent on the economic and political heft of the local magnate O'Brien. Undoubtedly, securing a conviction against Hurly was in the interest of O'Brien. Hurly's parallel legal campaign, although not alluded to during the trial, which sought to prove O'Brien's ongoing treasonous Jacobite activities, was undoubtedly a real and present danger to O'Brien's wealth and social status, his freedom and perhaps even, in a worst-case scenario, his life. As for the four accused, these accusations could become a matter of 'life or death'. For a short while at the end of 1700 there was a real possibility that O'Brien, a serving MP, would be charged with treason.

Why the trial resulted in a pamphlet war/skirmish is less clear. Why was Hurly first to enter the world of print and was this effusion subvented financially in some way? If we had sight of his first pamphlet, we might be able to gain some further, albeit perhaps oblique, access to his motivation. What seems clear is that O'Brien felt obliged to reply by publishing both the *Tryal* text and the *Appendix*. Presumably his aim was to demonstrate Hurly's scheming and heinous nature and his long-standing criminal intent. O'Brien's effusions into print in turn elicited Hurly's *Innocence Justify'd*. Engaging in mud-slinging pamphlet wars can be a dangerous strategy; some genuine evidence of wrongdoing might emerge and some of the mud might stick. In this instance the mutual slagging match did not add much to our store of knowledge.

What about the central figure of Patrick Hurly? There is little doubt that Hurly was a rogue and perhaps he could be characterized as a career criminal. As such, he may be *sui generis*, but in other ways he was emblematic of his age and of the dilemma facing some elements of the displaced Catholic elite in the aftermath of their, to all appearances, total defeat after the Treaty of Limerick. Not surprisingly, neither Hurly nor Joy have featured in the pantheon of nationalist, Catholic or rapparee resistance heroes; strictly speaking, they were not rapparees and, accordingly, as already noted, they have featured only occasionally in the historiography of the period. Perhaps their actions smack too much of criminality. Nevertheless, their escapades have not gone unnoticed. In particular, Ó Ciardha set the accusations against O'Brien in the context of the undoubtedly rather modest but not unimportant phenomenon of Protestant Jacobitism and in particular how 'the abortive invasion of 1692 provides a context for the witch-hunt against the Protestant landowner and Clare magnate Sir Donat O'Brien'.[5] He concluded that while the case was tainted by the use of disreputable witnesses, 'the discovery of personal conflicts does not always deprive such testimony of its value in reflecting an atmosphere of sedition from which it derives its credibility'.[6] Despite the implacable hostility of many members of the prosecution team to both to the Catholic interest and to the treaty articles, Eoin Kinsella has concluded that 'the Irish Privy Council (acting as a court of claims in 1692 and 1694), and the specially appointed judges who sat between 1697 and 1699, seemed to have adjudicated impartially'.[7] Can this climate of legal impartiality be extended to the Hurly trial and to the investigations into Hurly's allegations against O'Brien? There was certainly a sense of class solidarity and a reluctance to have O'Brien, one their own (even if in some respects he was 'damaged goods' because of his Gaelic and convert family background and his actions during the war) sacrificed on the evidence of the likes of Hurly. The O'Briens were no different from many of the Gaelic and Old English aristocratic families. Some, such as the Fingal branch of the Plunkett family, remained Catholic throughout the eighteenth century, as did Prestons Viscounts Gormanston and Brownes Viscounts Kenmare. All had significant and sometimes dominant Protestant elements within the family and, as the first duke of Ormond averred, religious differences 'dissolve not the obligation of nature' or, as Francis James, the leading historian of the eighteenth-century Irish House of Lords, expressed it somewhat more eloquently, 'nepotism often outweighed bigotry'.[8] Simms concluded that 'the relations between country gentlemen of different religions seem often to have been better than one would have supposed from the corporate actions of the Irish parliament'.[9]

Undoubtedly, Hurly was a thorough rogue, who by the spring of 1700 was in desperate financial trouble and who most likely did stage a sham robbery to claim the compensation under the rapparee acts. When that did not work, he may have turned informer as a career move; although it is also possible that he had already planned, in addition to the sham robbery, that he would turn king's evidence against his enemy O'Brien. But the very public nature of his challenge meant that the state authorities were galvanized to respond because they simply could not tolerate such an egregious and obviously mercenary attack, by a known Catholic Jacobite renegade, on a central plank of their security legislation. This is not to claim that the case against Hurly was brought because the authorities were concerned for the injury and the injustice that would have been inflicted on the innocent popish inhabitants of Clare. Hurly's resort to print probably took them by surprise. It was an even further challenge that needed to be met head on. The fact that the attack, the rebuttal and the counter-rebuttal were of such poor literary quality is a different issue; their existence is the important point.

The fragmentary sources on the life and times of Hurly are at times so improbable that they give rise to the suspicion that there may in fact have been more than one Patrick Hurly. Could it be the case that a collection of stories about a rather colourful Irishman had somehow been confused and conflated? It is certainly plausible that some of the actions attributed to him (forty wives and card sharping from King Louis XIV to the tune of 14,000 livres) were nothing more than a figment of a rampant journalistic imagination spreading scandalous and sensational fake news. On balance, however, it would appear that the sources referenced in this book and which can be cross-referenced and interlinked do refer to the same individual – Mr Patrick Hurly, Gentleman, of Moughna, Co. Clare, a minor Jacobite functionary, a serial cheat and fraudster, and a bigamist who was perused by the authorities in Ireland, England, France and Holland, convicted of perjury and fraud in Dublin on 31 May 1701, but who subsequently escaped from gaol, both in Dublin and in London, and who died suddenly while taking the air in Dublin Bay in January 1716 with the latest target for his bigamous schemes. He was buried 'in a Christian manner, which is more than he deserv'd', at St Mary's Church, Dublin.

Notes

ABBREVIATIONS

ESTC English Short Title Catalogue
IRA   Irish Republican Army
JP   Justice of the Peace
NLI   National Library of Ireland
TCD   Trinity College Dublin

INTRODUCTION

1 7 Will. III, c. 21 enacted in 1695 as amended and added to by 9 Will. III, c. 34 enacted in 1697. The Rapparees were Irish guerrilla fighters on the Royalist side during the Cromwellian conquest and the Jacobite side during the 1690s Williamite war.

2 While the term Protestant ascendancy was used for the first time in the 1780s, the term is sufficiently capacious and well-understood by historians to be used in the context of the last years of the seventeenth and the first decades of the eighteenth century.

3 These publications were *Patrick Hurly's vindication with some remarkable passages of his life and actions* (Dublin, 1701) (no copy has survived), *The tryal and conviction of Patrick Hurly, late of Moughna in the county of Clare, gent. in his majesty's court of Kings' Bench in Ireland, the 31st of May 1701* (Dublin, 1701), *The tryal and conviction of Patrick Hurly, late of Moughna in the county of Clare, gent. in his majesty's court of kings' bench in Ireland, the 31st of May 1701* (London, 1701), *An appendix being an answer to a libel intituled Patrick Hurly's vindication with some remarkable passages of his life and actions* (Dublin, 1701) and *Innocence Justify'd, or; The correction of an infamous libel called the Tryal & conviction of Patrick Hurly &c. published without license by Gunn, Whalley &c. together with a direct paragraphical answer to a most scandalous pamphlet entituled The appendix &c. suppos'd to be writ by order of Sir Donogh O'Bryen* (Dublin, 1701).

4 Thomas Wright, *History of Ireland* (Dublin, 1854), ii, pp 280–1.

5 J.G. Simms, *The Williamite confiscation in Ireland, 1690–1703* (London, 1956), pp 123–4.

6 James Comyn, *Irish at law* (London, 1983), pp 12–16.

7 Ciarán Ó Murchadha, 'The Moughna affair, 1699, and the bizarre career of Patrick Hurley', *The Other Clare*, 17 (1993), pp 48–56. Ó Murchadha incorrectly dated the robbery to 1699 as he failed to make allowance for the old-style dating conventions in which the new year was deemed to commence on 25 March.

8 There are two calendars of the Inchiquin Papers. See NLI Inchiquin Papers: www.nli.ie/sites/default/files/2022–12/143_inchiquin.pdf, last accessed 1 Mar. 2024 and a printed edition from the Irish Manuscripts Commission; John Ainsworth (ed.), *The Inchiquin manuscripts* (Dublin, 1961).

9 State Papers Ireland, SP63.

10 See later references to Patrick Hurly in chs 2 and 3.

11 *Dublin Evening Post*, 28–31 Jan. 1716.

12 Neal Garnham, *The courts, crime and the criminal law in Ireland, 1692–1700* (Dublin, 1996).

13 See T.D. Watt, *Popular protest and policing in ascendancy Ireland, 1691–1761* (Woodbridge, 2018), pp 104–28; S.J.

Connolly, 'Law, order and popular protest in early eighteenth-century Ireland: the case of the houghers' in P.J. Corish (ed.), *Radicals, rebels and establishment* (Belfast, 1985), p. 65.

1. PROTESTANT ASCENDANCY: CONSOLIDATING CONQUEST AND WINNING THE PEACE

1 For a detailed description of the war, see John Childs, *The Williamite wars in Ireland, 1688–1691* (London, 2007).
2 Patrick Walsh, *The making of the Irish Protestant ascendancy: the life of William Conolly, 1662–1729* (Dublin, 2010); Eoin Kinsella, *Catholic survival in Protestant Ireland, 1660–1711: Colonel John Browne, landownership and the Articles of Limerick* (Dublin, 2018).
3 See Daniel Corkery, *The hidden Ireland: a study of Gaelic Munster in the eighteenth century* (Dublin, 1925) for the classic presentation of this analysis; for an up-to-date review of some of the same material, see Vincent Morley, *The popular mind in eighteenth-century Ireland* (Cork, 2017).
4 See Kinsella, *Catholic survival*.
5 For recent scholarship on the Penal Laws, see John Bergin, Eoin Magennis, Lesa Ní Mhunghaile and Patrick Walsh (eds), *New perspectives on the Penal Laws* (Dublin, 2011).
6 See E.M. Johnston-Liik (ed.), *History of the Irish parliament, 1692–1800* (5 vols, Belfast, 2002) and Queen's University Belfast, Irish Legislation Database, www.qub.ac.uk/ild/?func=simple_search (accessed 1 Mar. 2024) and James Kelly with Mary Ann Lyons (eds), *The Proclamations of Ireland, 1660–1820* (5 vols, Dublin, 2014), ii.
7 7 William iii, c. 21.
8 C.I. McGrath, *The making of the eighteenth-century Irish constitution: government, parliament and the revenue, 1692–1714* (Dublin, 2000), p. 101.
9 F.J. Bigger, 'A Huguenot hero of Berhaven in 1704', *Journal of the Cork Historical and Archaeological Society*, 4:40 (1898), pp 287–307 at p. 307.
10 See Pádraigh Lenihan, 'The "Irish" Brigade, 1690–1715', *Eighteenth-Century Ireland*, 31 (2016), pp 47–74 and Pierre-Louis Coudray, *'More furies than men': the Irish Brigade in the service of France, 1690–1792* (London, 2022).
11 Neal Garnham, *The courts, crime and the criminal law in Ireland, 1692–1700* (Dublin, 1996); idem, 'Local elite creation in early Hanoverian Ireland: the case of the county grand jury', *Historical Journal*, xlii (1999), pp 623–42; David Fleming, *Politics and provincial people: Sligo and Limerick, 1691–1761* (Manchester, 2010); idem, 'Affection and disaffection in eighteenth-century mid-Munster Gaelic poetry', *Eighteenth-Century Ireland*, xxvii (2012), pp 84–98; T.D. Watt, *Popular protest and policing in ascendancy Ireland, 1691–1761* (Woodbridge, 2018).
12 For biographical detail on these MPs, see Johnston-Liik (ed.), *History of the Irish parliament*.
13 J.G. Simms, 'Irish Jacobites', *Analecta Hibernica*, 22 (1960), pp 11–187 at p. 15.
14 Éamonn Ó Ciarda, *Ireland and the Jacobite cause, 1685–1766: a fatal attachment* (Dublin, 2002), pp 108–9.
15 James Bonnell to Robert Harley, 3 Nov. 1691, *The manuscripts of the duke of Portland* (London, 1894), pp 479–81.
16 Simms, *Williamite confiscation*, pp 52, 2.
17 Ibid., p. 99.
18 *List of the claims as they are entered with the trustees at Chichester House on College-Green, Dublin, on or before the tenth of August, 1700* (Dublin, 1701). See Clare County Library, Chichester House list of claims, 1700, for the details of the 167 claims from Co. Clare: www.clarelibrary.ie/eolas/coclare/genealogy/chichester_house_claims_1700.htm (accessed 1 Sept. 2023).

2. GUILTY AS CHARGED? THE TRIAL AND CONVICTION OF PATRICK HURLY

1 *The tryal and conviction of Patrick Hurly, late of Moughna in the county of Clare, gent. in his majesty's court of Kings' Bench in Ireland, the 31st of May 1701.*
2 Colum Kenny, 'The Four Courts in Dublin before 1796', *Irish Jurist*, new series, 21:1 (summer 1986), pp 107–24 at pp 117–18.
3 See Kevin Whelan, 'An underground gentry? Catholic middlemen in eighteenth-century Ireland', *Eighteenth-*

century Ireland/Iris an dá chultúr, 10 (1995), pp 7–68.
4 Patrick Dineen, Focloir Gaedhlige agus Bearla / An Irish English dictionary (Dublin, 1927) and Logainm.ie www.logainm.ie/en/6815 (accessed 16 Sept. 2023).
5 Clare FM, 7 Mar. 2023, www.clare.fm/podcasts/townlands-focus-moughna (accessed 1 Oct. 2023).
6 The Down Survey of Ireland, TCD, http://downsurvey.tcd.ie/history.html (accessed 17 Sept. 2023).
7 Irish Examiner, 14 May 2018, www.irishexaminer.com/news/arid-30842845.html; History Ireland, 20:6, www.historyireland.com/missing-in-action.
8 List of the claims.
9 In the eighteenth century the term 'country' was often used when referring to a county.
10 Writs and executions were the technical terms for the serving of writs for debts due and for which the debtor could be imprisoned indefinitely. Instances of such imprisonment feature later in the text.
11 Registry of Deeds, 7/350/2659.
12 Mary Phelan, Irish speakers, interpreters and the courts, 1754–1921 (Dublin, 2019). Phelan claims that the use of interpreters was not unusual even from a relatively early date. She recorded that the earliest mention of a payment was in April 1754 to an Owen McConigall for work on Grand Jury presentments.
13 'O'Brien, Máire ("Máire Rua")', Maureen Murphy, Dictionary of Irish biography, available at www.dib.ie (accessed 10 Apr. 2024).
14 Registry of Deeds, 9/153/3412.
15 The Flying Post; or, The Postmaster, 17, 19 Dec. 1700.
16 London Gazette, 12 May 1709.
17 London Gazette, 20 Jan. 1711.
18 Dublin Evening Post, 28–31 Jan. 1716.
19 Biographical detail on Sir Donat is taken from Johnston-Liik (ed.), History of the Irish parliament, v, pp 366–7.
20 Clare County Library, Association for the Preservation of the Memorials of the Dead, Ireland www.clarelibrary.ie/eolas/coclare/genealogy/memorials/kilnasoolagh.htm, accessed 20 Feb. 2024.
21 'Aodh "Buí" Mac Crúitín', Vincent

Morley, available at www.dib.ie (accessed 10 Apr. 2024).

3. THE CASE OF PATRICK HURLY: IN LAW, IN POLITICS AND IN PRINT

1 John Langbein, 'The prosecutorial origins of defence counsel in the eighteenth century; the appearance of solicitors', Cambridge Law Journal, 58:2 (July 1999), pp 314–65 at p. 314.
2 Comyn, Irish at law, pp 12–16.
3 See James Oldham, 'Eighteenth-century judges' notes: how they explain, correct and enhance the reports', American Journal of Legal History, 31:1 (Jan. 1987), pp 9–42.
4 F.E. Ball, The judges in Ireland, 1221–1921 (2 vols, New York, 1927), ii, p. 18.
5 John Langbein, 'The criminal trial before the lawyers', University of Chicago Law Review, 45:2 (winter 1978), pp 263–316.
6 See James Oldham, 'Truth-telling in the eighteenth-century English courtroom', Law and History Review, 12:1 (spring 1994), pp 95–121 for a discussion of this issue.
7 See M.D. Gordon, 'The invention of a common law crime: perjury and the Elizabethan courts', American Journal of Legal History, 24:2 (Apr. 1980), pp 145–70.
8 Oldham, 'Truth-telling', p. 103.
9 The proceedings of the Old Bailey, London's Central Criminal Court, 1674–1913, www.oldbaileyonline.org/search.jsp?gen=1&form=searchHomePage&_divs_fulltext=perjury+affidavit&kwparse=and&start=0&count=0 (accessed 10 Sept. 2023).
10 Éamonn Ó Ciardha, Ireland and the Jacobite cause, 1685–1766: a fatal attachment (Dublin, 2002), passim.
11 For the feeble and easily foiled assassination plot, see Jane Garrett, The triumphs of providence (Cambridge, 1980).
12 Kinsella, Catholic survival, p. 242; Francis Brewster, A discourse concerning Ireland and the different interests thereof (London, 1698), pp 242, 22.
13 See Watt, Popular protest, passim, pp 120–1; M.W. Beresford, 'The common informer, the penal statutes and economic regulation', Economic History Review, new ser., x (1957), p. 21.
14 See Margaret Robinson, 'Treasons,

stratagems and spoils: Lancashire Plot, 1689–1694', *Contrebis: Journal of the Lancaster Archaeological and Historical Society*, 36 (2018), pp 50–3.
15 Rachel Weil, *A plague of informers: conspiracy and political trust in William III's England* (New Haven, CT, 2013).
16 See Ó Ciardha, *Ireland and the Jacobite cause* for a discussion of Jacobite conspiracies in Ireland in this period.
17 See Library of Congress, www.loc.gov/item/2021666765/ (accessed 1 Mar. 2024); Natasha Simonva, 'Owning the English rogue: commerce and reputation in restoration authorship', *Restoration: Studies in English Literary Culture, 1660–1700*, 40:1 (spring 2016), pp 67–84.
18 See John Gibney, *Ireland and the popish plot* (London, 2009).
19 See State trials: Bodleian Library, Subject and Research Guides, for the background to these publications: https://libguides.bodleian.ox.ac.uk/lawhistcom/sttr (accessed 11 Sept. 2023).
20 T.B. Howell (comp.), *A complete collection of state trials and proceedings for high treason and other crimes and misdemeanours* (London, 1816).
21 For a detailed review of political publishing in this period, see Suzanne Forbes, *Print and party politics in Ireland, 1689–1714* (London, 2018).
22 James Kelly, 'Health for sale: Mountebanks, doctors, printers and the supply of medication in eighteenth-century Ireland', *Proceedings of the Royal Irish Academy*, 108C (2008), pp 75–113.
23 Robert Munter, *The history of the Irish newspaper, 1685–1760* (Cambridge, 1967); M. Pollard, *A dictionary of members of the Dublin book trade, 1550–1800* (London, 2000); Forbes, *Print and party politics*.
24 Andrew Carpenter (ed.), John Dunton: *The Dublin scuffle* (Dublin, 2000), p. 170.
25 Francis Charteris (1665–1732) was a notorious Scottish-born gambler and rake. He was the inspiration for Hogarth's *A rake's progress*.
26 Theophilus Lucas, *The memoirs of the lives, intrigues and comical adventures of the most famous gamesters and celebrated sharpers in the reigns of Charles II, James II, William III and Queen Anne* (London, 1714).
27 *London Gazette*, 12 May 1709.
28 *Post Boy*, 19 May 1713.
29 *Post Boy*, 8 Oct. 1713.
30 *Rickard Burke, gent. and Elizabeth his wife, administratix of Patrick Hurley, gent, her former husband deceased … appellants. Christopher O'Brien esq. --- respondent, Et e contra. The first appellant's case* (London, 1725).

CONCLUSION

1 Wright, *History of Ireland*, ii, pp 280–1.
2 Simms, *Williamite confiscation*, pp 123–4; Ó Murchadha, 'The Moughna affair'.
3 Ball, *The judges in Ireland*, ii, p. 18.
4 Comyn, *Irish at law*, pp 12–16.
5 Ó Ciarda, *Ireland and the Jacobite cause*, p. 109.
6 Ibid., pp 108–9.
7 Kinsella, *Catholic survival*, pp 78–80.
8 Francis James, *Lords of the ascendancy: the Irish House of Lords and its members, 1600–1800* (Dublin, 1995), p. 93.
9 J.G. Simms, 'The Williamite forfeitures, 1690–1703' (PhD, TCD, 1952), p. 78.

Index

Act for the Better Suppression of Tories, Robbers and Rapparees (1695 and 1697) 9, 20, 27, 30, 35, 38, 75, 76, 80
Act of Resumption, 1700 25
An appendix being an answer to a libel intituled Patrick Hurly's vindication with some remarkable passages of his life and actions (Dublin, 1701) 12, 48, 52, 54, 66–71, 77
Anne, queen 28
Argent, William alias John Warner 62
Arthur, Sir Daniel 47
Arthur, Mr Thomas 31–3, 35, 38, 39, 59

Banks, Mr 22, 38
Beale, Mary 57
Bennis, Austin 29
Bernard, Francis 16, 23, 37, 38, 76
Bindon, David 10, 23, 37
Blood, Neptune 9, 23, 26, 27, 30, 40, 41
Bonnell, James 24
Bordeaux: Irish College 68
Boru, Brian 15, 48
Bourk, Thomas 35
Brady, Hugh 29
Brady, John 29
Brewster, Francis 63
Bridewell 48
Brodrick, Alan 11, 23, 30, 45, 54, 60, 63
Brown, Thomas 29, 30
Burke, Richard 72, 73
Burton, Francis 30
Butler, Mr 37, 41
Butler, Mr 50
Butler, Pierce 42, 72
Butler, Thomas 29
Butler, Toby 24, 30, 35, 41

Carbery, Co. Cork 66
Carty, Calaghan 31–3, 58
Carty, Daniel 31, 34, 37
Carty, Teige 31
Catholic elite 13, 15, 17–19, 21, 22, 24, 62, 67, 75, 77, 78
Cecil, Joseph 29
Chalmers, George 29

Charteris, Francis 47, 72
Clare, Lord (Charles O'Brien) 30, 47
Commission of Inquiry into the Forfeited Estates in Ireland 25, 30, 43, 50, 62, 69
Cooper, John 15, 48, 69
Coneene, Margaret alias Peggy Rabbett 33, 34
Connell, Patrick 29, 30
Coote, Thomas 40, 45, 46, 58, 59, 63
Crips, John 33, 40, 41, 61
Cusak, James 23, 39, 41, 42

Daly, Denis 24, 47
Deane, Elizabeth 50
de Massue, Henri, 2nd marquis de Ruvigny, earl of Galway 42, 64
Drew, John 29, 30
Dromoland, Co. Clare 11, 50, 57,
Dublin: Blackhorse Avenue 29; Chichester House 30; Christ Church Yard 27; Marshalsea prison 29, 63; St Mary's Church 47, 48, 79

Ennis, Co. Clare, gaol and assizes 11, 21, 29, 32, 35, 44, 61

Fontaine, James 21
Foster, John 23, 40
Finch, Daniel (2nd earl of Nottingham) 28, 65
FitzGerald, Augustine 23, 29
FitzSimons, Charles 39

Galway, earl of, Henri De Massue, 2nd marquis de Ruvigny, 42, 64
Gunne (Gun), Matthew 66, 71, 72
Guzman d'Alfrach Lazarillo de Tormes 69

Hamilton, George 50
Hamilton, Lucia 50
Handcock, William 23
Harley, Robert 24
Hart, William 72
Head, Richard 69
Hely, John 42

Index

Henn, Richard 29, 30
Hewlet, Thomas 43
Hickey, Daniel 30, 31, 37, 67
Hickey (Hicky), Mrs 37, 39, 61
Hickman, George 23, 39, 41
Hickman, Henry 30
Hickman, Thomas 23, 29, 42
Hickman, William 72
Hurly, Elizabeth 33, 39, 65, 72, 73
Hurly, John 23
Hurly, John 33, 37, 39, 45, 63
Hurly, John 8, 23, 28, 29, 37, 39, 41, 67
Hurly, Richard 38

Ikerin, Lord, Pierce Butler 42, 72
Inchiquin Papers 7, 10, 14–16, 26, 33, 35, 36, 41, 43, 48, 63, 69, 74, 75, 80
Ingoldsby, Henry 48, 69
Innocence Justify'd or, the correction of an Infamous libel, called the Tryal & Conviction of Patrick Hurly, &c. Published without License by Gunn, Whalley, &c. together, with a direct Paragraphical Answer, to a most Scandalous Pamphlet, Entituled, The Appendix &c. suppos'd to be Writ by Order of Sir Donogh O'Bryen (Dublin, 1701) 12, 30, 38, 48, 53, 54, 66, 69, 71, 77

Jacobite/Jacobitism 9, 10, 13–16, 18, 19, 22, 23, 28, 32, 41, 44, 45, 48, 49, 52, 62–4, 67, 71, 75–9
James II, king 47, 49, 68, 69
Jervis, Humphry 41
Johnson, Edward 47
Joy, Redmond 19, 61, 63–5, 77

Keightly, Thomas 50
Kemp, Dorothy 33, 39, 40
Kilnassoolagh, Co. Clare 50

La Hogue, France 22, 44, 62, 68
Leamaneh, Co. Clare 15, 48, 50, 57
Lloyd (Lloid) 64
Lovet, Col. 39
Lynch, Capt. 21, 37–40, 54, 61, 76

MacCarthy, Reagh 66
MacDonough, Charles 32, 35
MacMahon, Denis 29
Malone, Corporal 32
Malone, Edmund 25
McCaie/McCay, Daniel 31, 40
MacCollogby, Mortogh 33, 37, 61
MacCrúitín, Aodh Buí 50

McCarthy, Charles 44, 45
McDonogh, Timothy 70
McDonough, Bernard 50
McGonigall, Owen 82
McMahon, Matthew 70
McMahon 44
McDonnel, James 29, 30
McDonnell, Randal 44
McMahon, Máire Rua 15, 35, 48, 69
Meade, Sir John 23, 58
Mealing, Edward 29
Moughna, Co. Clare 7, 9, 28, 29, 33, 67, 79
Mountcallan (Montcallan), Viscount or Count 14, 29, 68, 69
Murihilly 67

Newmarket-on-Fergus, Co. Clare 50
Neylan, Daniel 35, 69
Neylan, Walter 35, 40, 42, 59

O'Brien, Mr 34
O'Brien, Conor 15, 48
O'Brien, Charles 44, 47
O'Brien, Christopher 40, 44, 72
O'Brien Andrews, Donough 31, 35, 58
O'Brien, Sir Donat 7, 8, 11–15, 18, 22, 24–6, 30, 34, 35, 37, 38, 41–9, 54–7, 62–71, 74, 76–8
O'Brien, Henry 50
O'Brien, Lucius 41, 43, 50
O'Brien, Murrough 39
O'Brien, Timothy 42
O'Bryan, Dermot 29

Patrick Hurly's vindication with some remarkable passages on his life and actions (Dublin, 1701) 12, 70
Penal Laws 13, 18, 20, 74
Perry, Edmund 29, 30
Protestant elite 11, 17, 22, 80
Privy Council 44, 45, 56, 78
Pyne, Richard 22, 32, 38, 41, 46, 65

Quin, Thady 64

Rabbett, Peggy 33, 34
Rice, Stephen 24
Roch(e), Richard 29, 63
Rochfort, Robert 11, 22, 23, 31, 32, 34, 42, 63
Ronane, Mr 9, 27, 33
Ronane, John 33
Ryswick, Peace of 1697 46
Ryves, Richard 22

Shovell, Daniel 72
St Germaine, court of King James 18, 19, 22
Southwell, Edward 28, 65

Talbot, Richard, 1st Earl of Tyrconnell 49
The tryal and conviction of Patrick Hurly: Late of Moughna in the county of Clare, Gent. In His Majesty's Court of Kings' Bench in Ireland, the 31st of May 1701 (Dublin, 1701) 12, 13, 15, 26, 29, 30, 33, 34, 37, 38, 47, 51, 54, 56, 60, 61, 66, 67, 70, 71, 75, 77
The tryal and conviction of Patrick Hurly: Late of Moughna in the county of Clare, Gent. In His Majesty's Court of Kings' Bench in Ireland, the 31st of May 1701 (London, 1701) 12
Tories/Rapparees 18–22, 39, 47, 80
Treaty/Articles of Galway 19, 24, 63
Treaty/Articles of Limerick 19, 24, 42, 63, 77
Trustees for the Sale of Forfeited Estates 25, 30, 43, 69
Twiford, Samuel 55
Tyrconnell, 1st Earl, Richard Talbot 49

Vernon, James 44–6, 64

Walton, Samuel 60
Wybrants, Daniel 44
Whalley, John 66, 71, 72